The Kit-Kat
Book of Fun F...

Susie Boulton

Scotland

Northumbria

Cumbria

Yorkshire
and
Humberside

The
North
West

East Midlands

Wales

Heart of
England

East Anglia

Thames and
Chilterns

South
of
England

London and the
South East

The West Country

MARTIN BOOKS

CONTENTS

Published by Martin Books,
Simon & Schuster International Group
Fitzwilliam House,
32 Trumpington Street,
Cambridge CB2 1QY

First published 1988
© Woodhead-Faulkner (Publishers) Ltd 1988
ISBN 0 85941 454X

Printed in Spain.

FOREWORD

It is with great pleasure that I introduce this *KitKat Book of Fun Family Outings*.

In producing it, our aim has been to provide a guide that is both detailed and honest, giving basic – but vital – information on some of the many thousands of family attractions in which our country abounds.

We hope that it will not only enable you to plan your days out more successfully, but also introduce you to attractions that you have not heard of before, providing the basis for many happy family outings.

A. M. Marsh
Director, Rowntree Mackintosh Confectionery Ltd

ABOUT THE AUTHOR

Susie Boulton has travelled extensively and is now a freelance travel writer, contributing to national magazines and newspapers. She has previously written guidebooks on France and Italy. She worked for *Holiday Which?* for ten years and has experience of a wide range of leisure and holiday activities. She lives in Cambridge with her husband and young son.

ACKNOWLEDGEMENTS

The author and publishers would like to thank the following places for permission to reproduce the photographs in this book:
Alton Towers
Chessington World of Adventures
The National Maritime Museum, Greenwich
The National Motor Museum, Beaulieu
Mark Wilkinson and the Dart Valley Steam Railway
The Imperial War Museum, Duxford
Whipsnade Park Zoo, Dunstable
Longdale Rural Craft Centre
West Midlands Safari and Leisure Park
Caernarfon Castle
Jorvik Viking Centre, York
Beamish North of England Open-air Museum
Wigan Pier Heritage Centre
Holker Hall, Cumbria
Edinburgh Butterfly Farm

INTRODUCTION

The choice of family attractions in Britain is now bigger than ever before. Mansions and monuments; theme parks and pleasure parks; galleries and gardens; castles and country parks; these are just a few of the attractions that you can find throughout the country. When it comes to a family outing, it's not just a question of passive viewing: you can ride a steam railway, step on to Concorde, spot a Golden Eagle, throw and paint a pot or make a scarecrow. There's something for everyone, from tiny tots to sprightly grannies.

It's one thing to know about all the attractions available, however, it's another to organise an outing and ensure that everyone gets the most out of it. So many family outings fail to live up to expectations because it pours with rain, or because the castle is closed or just because the baby's nappies were left behind. There *is* no magic recipe for the perfect day out: you can't guarantee the sunshine or the fact the toddler won't wail all day. But a little planning in advance can make a surprisingly big contribution to the success of a day's outing: that's what I hope to explain in this book.

The advice in this book is based on my own experiences, both as a travel journalist and researcher and as organiser of family outings for several years. I've had my share of near-disasters – at least on the family front – such as losing a toddler in a deer park and a stepson in a theme park; and I've left the buggy at home on more than one occasion. Nevertheless I've decided that, on balance, day trips with children are more fun and rewarding than those without them.

The book is divided into two sections. The first helps you plan the outing and eliminate all the potential hitches: it tells you what to pack in the bags, how to keep the kids amused on the journey and how to help them get the most out of the place you visit. After this comes a gazetteer of places to visit. It is divided into the English Tourist Board regions and gives all the practical information you're likely to need, such as facilities provided, the costs, opening hours and so on. There are no excuses now for sitting at home on high days and holidays, listening to the moans and groans of perpetually bored youngsters. There's a wealth of family attractions waiting to be discovered, so pack up Granny, the kids and the KitKats and make the most of the break!

OUTINGS WITH FAMILY APPEAL

Family outings are not just fun, they can be educational too. A steam railway, a stately home, a zoo or a museum: all these are places where children and adults can discover, experiment and learn.

The almost proverbial museum full of dusty cabinets containing dreary relics is fast disappearing. More and more museums and galleries are getting rid of their stuffy image and becoming increasingly accessible and interesting to children. Take some of the big sights in London: the Science Museum has displays controlled by knobs to press, and models to operate; children's quizzes with weekly prizes; and the new Launch Pad where children as young as three years old can join in the demonstrations of physics principles. At the Natural History Museum, children can handle a python skin, touch fossils and bones and study a butterfly wing through a microscope.

It's not just the big sights in London that offer so much scope for children. All over the country you can find museums that provide special facilities for children, as well as historic houses that bring history alive for them, perhaps by providing special guided tours for the young or characters in mediaeval costumes to welcome visitors.

Stately homes these days are more than country mansions with collections of paintings, porcelain and furniture. In the larger ones you may find a miniature railway, a museum of veteran cars or an adventure playground for children.

Activities provided during school summer holidays are particularly varied. There are museums where children can make things as diverse as lavender bags, scarecrows, gingerbread, baskets and Easter bonnets. Check the gazetteer entries for your region, find out about local craft centres and ask your local tourist board (addresses on pages 15–16) for details.

There are lots of ways in which you can help your children make the most of an outing. Most youngsters don't object to sightseeing on principle, particularly if there are a few ice creams or home-made scones to look forward to.

If it's a cultural trip, such as one to a historic house, museum or exhibition, try giving them a few simple explanations of who lived there and the kind of sight they can expect before you set off; and provide them each with a pencil and pad to jot down their favourite painting or exhibit. If there are worksheets available, encourage children to fill them in: but on no account force them to do so. You don't want to turn the visit into a competition.

Encourage children to take photos, either with a cheap instamatic camera of their own or with yours if you can lend it to them for a shot or two. Some of the larger attractions will even hire out cameras, but remember that film bought there will be very expensive. Most children are quite keen photographers once you've shown them the basic rules. The prints they take will be a good way of helping them to remember the day out.

What most children won't remember are long lists of dates and historical facts, so don't expect them to churn out the contents of the guided tour on the way home. As long as they remember some little detail about the day's outing – even if it's only the peacocks in the park – then it's a worthwhile trip.

Some planning in advance is crucial to the success of the outing, particularly if it's going to be fun for all the members of the family. Firstly, what style of outing is going to suit you best? The peace and quiet of a solitary castle, or a thrilling, action-packed day in a gigantic, Disney-style theme park? A deserted nature reserve or the historic sights of a bustling city?

Ideally, the outing should be geared to all members of the family. This isn't necessarily easy if there are big gaps between the ages of the children. One answer to the problem is to choose some attraction where the family can split up; for example, at a suitable stately home Mum could take the eight year-olds on a guided tour of the manor while Dad and the four-year-old have fun looking at the veteran cars and model railways. Outings can be fun for grandparents too; they can point out and explain to grandchildren all the things that functioned in their day, from mangles to steam engines.

Before finally deciding on your destination, you need to give plenty of thought to the facilities provided. Some attractions have a whole range of facilities, from souvenir shops and ice cream kiosks to adventure playgrounds, while some delightful but isolated ones may not be able to offer even a cup of tea. Consider the stamina, needs and dislikes of each party member.

Perennial hits with all members of the family, and particularly the young ones, are zoos and wildlife parks: the very thought of glimpsing a real lion or rhino fills most children with delight. Again some sort of forward-planning is a good idea. What sort of park will suit you and the family best? A tiny local zoo, a nature reserve, a butterfly centre, an aquarium, a wildlife or a safari park? Outings can range from the exotic parks of Windsor, Longleat and Woburn, where you can admire rare Siberian tigers, bongo antelopes or lions lounging under trees, to tiny, informal zoos, costing a fraction of the price, which feature more familiar but not necessarily less interesting species. All of them make for interesting days out, provided you've thought about practicalities; for instance, feeding times and special displays only happen once a day, usually in the afternoons. And it may sound obvious, but do remember that most zoos and animal parks really aren't much fun in the rain.

Worth thinking about as an alternative to a zoo is a farm park or country museum, which will normally feature live animals such as pigs, cattle, hens, ducks and geese, as well as exhibitions of rural farming crafts showing how foods like butter and flour were made by hand. It's a joy to watch children react to the simple pleasures of a farmyard – feeding the piglets or billy goats, stroking a rabbit or even riding a real tractor. These sort of museums can be found all over the country and they're particularly popular with children brought up in towns and cities, who have little experience of the rural way of life. It's easy to forget that just to see a chicken pecking around in the open these days can be a delightful novelty for a city child.

The latest additions to British family attractions are the big theme and pleasure parks, which provide fun days out for all the family. There is usually a selection of rides to suit all the family's tastes, as well as shows, live entertainments museums and displays. Entrance charges to theme parks are high, but they are inclusive prices which allow you to try as many things as you like; they represent good value for money for energetic families.

The popularity of theme parks means that crowds and queues are inevitable at bank holidays and summer weekends. Some provide entertainment such as buskers to enliven the queuing, but it might be a good idea to be prepared with some ideas of your own. Some of the games for playing in the car on pages 11–12 could be a help. Another good idea is to pack the children's personal stereos, if they have them, with some tapes that haven't already been heard in the car.

Whatever attraction you choose, a little thought about making it fun for all the family, and a little planning, can make all the difference to the success of your day.

HOW TO SURVIVE
THE JOURNEY

Travelling is all part of the fun of a family outing, or at least it should be. First, you have all the excitement of packing up and setting off; then there's that first, thrilling glimpse of the seaside, the castle on the clifftop or the rhino in the zoo.

We all know, however, that travelling can be the most tedious part of the whole day's outing as children bored by being cooped up in the back of cars can make themselves and everyone else completely miserable. Fortunately, there are lots of ways that parents can make travelling more fun for everyone. One obvious tip is to cut down travelling to the minimum. Pick up a regional guide to your area and you might find there's something fun to see or do surprisingly close to home. If, on the other hand, the family attraction that everyone wants to see is far from home, you have to choose between two possibilities. Either you get there as fast as you can, ignoring all the moans from the back of the car; or you plan your journey to have plenty of stops to allow youngsters to stretch their legs and let off steam.

Whichever you choose, you'll need something to relieve the monotony of the journey. For the moment, we'll assume you're going by car and that a bag of boredom-relievers won't cramp your style.

Snacks and drinks for all members of the party are essential. Apples, pears and other fruit; crisps; nuts; muesli bars; chocolate bars and biscuits; all these will be welcome. Don't forget fruit juice: orange is universally popular, but the individual packs that come with their own straw allow you to buy everyone's favourite flavour and are easy to drink from as well.

Though snacks and nibbles do a lot to enliven the journey, however, you'll need to think of more than food to relieve boredom, at least on longer journeys. Try games, quizzes, and jokes, or cassettes with stories, fairytales or music. Your local branch of W.H. Smith should give you plenty of ideas. They stock a good selection of paperback books giving ideas for travelling with children, as well as a wide range of suitable tapes; there are even a couple of cassettes for new-born babies that imitate the sounds of the womb and send the baby to sleep! According to the surveys these are remarkably successful.

If a book or cassette is an extra whose cost you hadn't counted in that of the outing, here are a few free ideas: all of them are games that I've found are a big hit with all but very tiny members of the family.

Cats and Dogs

This is a good one for all ages and especially good if you're driving through built-up areas. You score one point for spotting a dog, two for a cat, three for a dog in a car and ten for a cat in a car. The player with the most points at the end of the journey wins.

Heads and Legs

This game is based on the names of pubs. You score one point for spotting a leg on the sign of a pub and one for a head; so the Green Man gets three points (two legs and a head), the Red Lion five (four legs and a head) and the Fox and Goose eight (six legs and two heads).

A–Z of the roadside

A variation on I-Spy. Instead of spotting objects beginning with one letter only, you move through the alphabet as fast as you can. You first have to spot something beginning with the letter A (e.g., apple tree), then you move on to B (bridge, bicycle, butcher), then to C and so on.

Number-plate anagrams

Take the three letters from the number plate of the car in front and use them in any order to make the shortest (or longest word) you can. So, for example, if it's XEB you could go for 'boxer'; MXU could become 'exhume'. This is not suitable for very young children.

Associations

The first player thinks of a noun and the second says the first word that comes into his or her head which is associated with the first word. The third player does likewise, thinking of a word associated with the second player's word and so on. The game has to move fast and any player who hesitates is 'out'. A typical game might go like this: 'apple/tree/Christmas/carol/church/steeple . . .'.

Number-plate sentences

Short sentences or phrases are made with the letters from the number plate taken from a car on the road. GTB might produce Go to Bed, EOM Early One Morning, and so on.

Rhymes

This is a good one for very little children. Players have to think of words which rhyme with the first chosen word, but it's not necessary to have the same number of syllables in the word. The first person might choose CAT, the second MAT, the third CHAT, the fourth BATTLE and so on. From very small children you could accept sounds rather than words.

Making words

Players take turns to suggest letters to make words. The first person might suggest I, the second M, the third (thinking of the word 'impossible') P, the fourth E (thinking of the word 'impenetrable') and so on. It soon becomes obvious what the word is to be and the player who ends the word is out. The key is to turn a word which is about to end into something longer, for example, 'impenetrable' can become 'impenetrability'.

Buzz and fuzz

This is a counting game in which every time the number 5 comes up (or multiples such as 15, 20, etc.) the word 'buzz' has to be substituted and every 7 (or multiples such as 14, 21, etc.) is replaced by the word 'fuzz'. Players take it in turns to count and anyone who says a number instead of a buzz or a fuzz, or says fuzz instead of buzz, loses a life. You have 9 lives to start with. Guaranteed to get a lot of laughs.

Spotter games with emphasis on the natural world are always great family favourites. Watch out for kestrels hovering, for mice on motorway roadsides and for rooks digging for grubs in ploughed fields or roosting together in tall trees. You can buy books to give you other ideas, for instance Usborne do a series of Spotter guides on subjects such as trees, birds and wild flowers.

One of the best buys in our family for long journeys was the Living and Learning lotto game of Animal Soundtracks. The aim is to match up the animal noises on tape with the photographs on the lotto boards, but just listening to the life-like grunts, roars, croaks and miaows can provide young children with hours of fun. The other game in the series, just called Sound Tracks, has a wider variety of noises, from the tick-tock of a clock to the crowing of a cockerel. Both are available from Early Learning Centres and main toy stores.

The easiest travellers of all are babies of six months and under, who have a wonderful habit of falling fast asleep once the engine is switched on. (So effective is the noise and motion of the car that some mothers find themselves driving round the block at night as the only means of getting the baby to go to sleep!) There are, of course, always exceptions: at six months, our toddler used to screech continuously in the back of the car. The problem was eventually solved by the installation of a cassette player and some soothing tapes, and the provision of a very liberal supply of milk and snacks.

The hardest age group to deal with on long car journeys is probably the one to five-year-olds, whose boredom threshold is particularly low. Once toddlers can talk they will invariably pose that perennial question-cum-complaint: 'How many more miles to go, Mummy?' Over-fives are easier to entertain and not nearly so fidgety, but if anyone suffers from carsickness they're likely to be the ones. Some ideas for preventing carsickness are on page 12.

For most children (but certainly *not* those prone to carsickness) one of the highlights of the journey is a meal en route. This may not be your own idea of the ideal lunch out, but a burger or some other junk food may be the price of a quiet and trouble-free journey. The Little Chef restaurants, for example, offer special menus and portions for children, as well as highchairs and playgrounds, and some even sell baby food and changing packs for babies, containing nappies, baby wipes and a couple of plastic bags. Other names to look out for are the Happy Eater restaurants and Granada service stations, which have imaginative outdoor play areas.

The expense of these sort of places does mount up, however, and you may prefer the much cheaper alternative of taking your own picnic. All you really need is a few sandwiches (egg, marmite and cheese spread are usually popular with children), fruit and cheese, crisps and some little treat at the end. It's often best to have the picnic at your destination. Many of the places I've listed in the gazetteer have delightful grounds for picnics, some equipped with tables and benches. Some also have their own catering facilities such as cafés, bars, restaurants or tea rooms but be prepared for queues and high prices.

Even though I am a well seasoned traveller, I have always found a check-list indispensable. Even those who are used to packing up the car for all the family find that it's easy to forget some small but crucial item, such as the baby's bottle or the toddler's favourite cuddly toy. Here, then, is a check-list drawn up from several years' experience of family outings, with children of all ages in mind:

Disposable nappies
Babywipes or moist sponge
Plastic bags (for nappies)
Baby's bottle or beaker
Rusks
Change of clothes for baby
Bib, bowl, spoon
Favourite cuddly toy
Box of tissues
Buggy or sling
Potty
Straps for highchair
Reins

Toys and games for toddlers
Snacks and drinks
Thermos of tea or coffee
Pen and notebook
Camera and film
Picnic
Rug for picnic
Sunglasses
Cassettes for the car
Suncream and sunblock
First aid box

The contents of a first aid box will vary from family to family, but the following list contains all the basic necessities:

Plasters	Antiseptic cream
Bandages	Calamine lotion
Scissors	Aspirin or paracetamol that is
Safety pins	suitable for children
Insect repellant spray	

Carsickness

Unfortunately, some children will suffer from carsickness whatever precautions you take, and in their case, the shorter you make the journey, the better. In the majority of children, though, carsickness can be prevented or cured. The following are a few tips:

- Don't give children who are prone to sickness greasy or rich food before setting off.
- Keep air circulating in the car.
- Keep the child's mind off the subject of sickness.
- Make frequent stops.
- Don't drive fast round bends.

By all means give children travel sickness pills if necessary, but bear in mind that some brands will make them drowsy and thirsty.

TRAVELLING BY PUBLIC TRANSPORT

Many of the most well known sights in the country, and quite a few of the minor ones, can be reached by coach or rail, or through an organised excursion and the joy of this, of course, is that somebody else drives while you sit back and enjoy the ride.

Travelling by train still has an element of excitement for youngsters, and it doesn't have to work out a lot more expensive than going by car. British Rail offers all sorts of discounts and there are family railcards which currently allow a third or more off all standard class (formerly second-class) fares. At the moment, these railcards allow up to four children to travel with the railcard-holder, for a flat return fare of just £1 per child. Cheap Day Returns are available throughout the country at any time at weekends, Bank Holidays and after the morning rush on weekdays (but remember that British Rail services on Sundays are much less frequent and can be disrupted by engineering work). 'Rover' tickets are worth considering if you're on holiday and want to go by train: they allow you to travel as much and as often as you like, for a week, in a given area. British Rail also offer special day trips to towns and other places of particular touristic interest. Ask at your local station or British Rail Travel Centre for details.

Travelling by coach nearly always works out a good deal cheaper than going by rail, but on the ordinary services the seats don't give you much leg- or elbow-room and you don't get the sort of facilities, such as loos and refreshments, that you find on trains. National Express links up most parts of the country with regular express coaches; some routes have Luxury Rapide coaches. Details are available from any National Express agent, or you can look up the local National Express number in the yellow pages or Thomson Local Directory. For general information and trips from London, ring the main office on 01 730 0202. There are additional services run by independent operators: again check in yellow pages, local papers or your Thomson Local Directory. The most expensive services are very well equipped, offering refreshments, reclining seats, lavatories and video entertainment. The cheaper the ticket, the more basic the facilities.

HOW MUCH WILL IT COST?

Entrance charges at some of the top attractions can be prohibitively expensive, especially if you are a large family. There are, of course, many family attractions that won't cost you a fortune, and even some that are free. Unlike many other countries, Britain still has hundreds of museums and galleries that make no admission charge. Some of the greatest treasure-houses of London – the British Museum, the National Gallery and the Science Museum – are all free, for example. Charges for other attractions, such as stately homes, zoos and country parks, vary widely. It's certainly worth checking the prices before you set off. Some places offer 'family tickets' that give substantial reductions; others have special discounts on certain days of the week or special off-season prices. Nearly all the attractions offer a big reduction for children which very often is half price for 3–14/15/16-year-olds and free entrance for toddlers. There are frequently special rates for Pensioners too; commonly, they are charged the same price as children, or a figure somewhere between the adult and child rates.

At stately homes, it's worth remembering that you can often just pay to see the grounds. Paying the extra for a lengthy guided tour of the house may be a waste of money if your family includes a toddler or a teenager who isn't interested. Sometimes castles and old houses are very sparsely furnished and the best parts are the façade and the garden.

As a family, our best investment has been membership of the National Trust. The Trust owns 250 properties throughout the country, many of them very fine stately homes. Currently, family membership (husband, wife and children from 5–18) costs £30, and entitles you to free entrance to all the properties. This means that a family of two adults and three children only has to make about three outings in a year to recoup the cost of the card. With membership, you receive the annual National Trust handbook, which gives factual details about all Trust properties throughout the country. To apply, write to:

The National Trust
Membership Department
P.O. Box 39
Bromley
Kent BR1 1NH,
or ask for details at any of their properties.

Also worth thinking about is membership of English Heritage, an organisation that cares for over 350 properties in the country, from Stonehenge and Hadrian's Wall to castles and industrial monuments. You can make substantial savings if you intend to visit several properties in a year. Current costs are £10 for individual membership, £20 for a family group, including all children under 16, and £6 for Pensioners. Membership entitles you to free admission to any of the properties, a free, fully illustrated guide book, a location map and a quarterly newsletter. Information from some tourist information centres or by post from:

English Heritage
Membership Department
P.O. Box 43
Ruislip
Middlesex

Another worthwhile organisation is the Historic Houses Association. By becoming a member you can help preserve some of Britain's finest houses, parks and gardens, while enjoying free access to over 260 of them.

Details from:
Membership Department
Historic Houses Association
P.O. Box 21
71 Keys Avenue
Letchworth
Herts SG6 3EY

The Royal Society for Nature Conservation has a junior branch, WATCH, which arranges a host of environment- and nature-centred activities for under-eighteens. Members receive a thrice-yearly magazine and for family outings such helpful things as nature guides for expeditions are available. Details from the Society at:

The Green
Nettleham
Lincoln LN2 2NR

Your children might also be interested in the following organisations, which have country-wide networks of branches with a variety of activities:

Young Archaeologists' Club
Dr Kate Pretty
New Hall College
Cambridge CB3 0DF

Young Ornithologists' Club
The Lodge
Sandy
Bedfordshire SG19 2DL

OTHER INFORMATION

TOURIST INFORMATION

The best sources for general information on family outings are the regional tourist boards. These cover the whole country and all the main ones publish an annual guide to their regional attractions, packed with information. At £1–£2 a copy, they are well worth buying, particularly if you're planning several outings.

In addition to these regional tourist boards, there are over seven hundred Tourist Information Centres throughout Britain. All of them welcome personal callers, whether locals or holidaymakers and whether you have an hour or a fortnight to spare for sightseeing. Each centre is well stocked with brochures, pamphlets and guides (both free and for sale) and staff can provide information on attractions within a radius of fifty miles of their centre or within the scope of a day's excursion.

REGIONAL TOURIST BOARDS

Cumbria Tourist Board
Ashleigh, Holly Road, Windermere,
Cumbria LA23 2AQ
Tel: 096 62 4444

East Anglia Tourist Board
(Cambridgeshire, Essex, Norfolk
and Suffolk)
14 Toppesfield Hall, Hadleigh,
Suffolk IP7 5DN
Tel: 0473 822922

East Midlands Tourist Board
(Derbyshire, Leicestershire,
Lincolnshire, Northamptonshire and
Nottinghamshire)
Exchequergate
Lincoln LN2 1PZ
Tel: 0522 531521

Heart of England Tourist Board
(Gloucestershire, Herefordshire,
Shropshire, Staffordshire,
Warwickshire, Worcestershire and
West Midlands)
2–4 Trinity Street
Worcester WR1 2PW
Tel: 0905 613132

**London Tourist Board and
Convention Bureau**
(Greater London area)
26 Grosvenor Gardens
London SW1W 0DU
Tel: 01 730 3488

North West Tourist Board
(Cheshire, Greater Manchester,
Lancashire, Merseyside and High
Peak District of Derbyshire)
The Last Drop Village
Bromley Cross, Bolton
Lancashire BL7 9PZ
Tel: 0204 591511

Northumbria Tourist Board
(Cleveland, Durham,
Northumberland and Tyne and
Wear)
Aykley Heads
Durham DH1 5UX
Tel: 091 384 6905

Scotland Tourist Board
23 Ravelston Terrace
Edinburgh EH4 3EU
Tel: 031 332 2433

South East England Tourist Board
(East Sussex, Kent, Surrey and West
Sussex)
1 Warwick Park
Tunbridge Wells, Kent TN2 5TA
Tel: 0892 40766

Southern Tourist Board
(Hampshire, Eastern and Northern
Dorset and Isle of Wight)
Town Hall Centre
Leigh Road, Eastleigh
Hampshire SO5 4DE
Tel: 0703 616027

Thames & Chilterns Tourist Board
(Bedfordshire, Berkshire,
Buckinghamshire, Hertfordshire and
Oxfordshire)
8 The Market Place
Abingdon, Oxfordshire
OX14 3UD
Tel: 0235 22711

Wales Tourist Board
Brunel House
2 Fitzalan Road
Cardiff CF2 1UY
Tel: 0222 499909
(Office also at 34 Piccadilly, London
W1. Tel: 01 409 0969)

West Country Tourist Board
(Avon, Cornwall, Devon, West
Dorset, Somerset, Wiltshire and
Scilly Isles)
Trinity Court
37 Southernhay East
Exeter, Devon EX1 1QS
Tel: 0392 76351

**Yorkshire & Humberside Tourist
Board** (North, South, West
Yorkshire and Humberside)
312 Tadcaster Road,
York YO2 2HF
Tel: 0904 707961

WINTER OPENING

Most people think of family outings as summer events, but there is no reason why you shouldn't choose to go off-season. It is true that many of the attractions (including all the theme parks and the majority of stately homes) are closed for the winter, but there are more places open than you might imagine. Most zoos, wildlife parks and a number of castles and museums are open every day of the year except at Christmas and perhaps New Year. Some historic properties are open in winter, though normally on only certain days and at restricted times. Woburn Abbey, Windsor Castle, Leeds Castle and Castle Howard are just a few of the famous attractions which are open all year. Most National Trust properties close for winter, but some of them open their shops during November and December for Christmas shoppers. Their shops are particularly attractive, and buying presents in them could be a pleasant change from your local high street.

For any serious lover of art and architecture, winter is the ideal time for cultural visits. No traffic jams on the way, no crowds or parking problems once you arrive. Contact the relevant Tourist Board and they will tell you what is open in the area you are interested in.

THE DISABLED

Many of the family attractions in this book are accessible or partly accessible to the disabled. Where there are special facilities or no problems for a wheelchair, the symbol ⑁ has been inserted in the individual entries of the gazetteer plus any relevant comments. It is advisable, however, to ring the site before a visit and find out about the facilities. The National Trust annually publishes a useful free booklet which gives details of special facilities for the disabled at National Trust properties. It is available by post from:

The National Trust
P.O. Box 39
Bromley
Kent BR1 1NH

Note: Details of attractions and prices given in this book were the most up-to-date available at the time of going to press. Actual features, opening times and admission prices may differ from those given. Readers should telephone to check on these details, especially if variations would cause disappointment. Whilst every care has been taken to ensure the accuracy of the information, no liability for any errors and omissions can be accepted by the author, the publishers or the Rowntree Group of Companies.

LONDON AND THE SOUTH EAST

London Zoo
British Museum
Planetarium
Madame Tussaud's
Museum of London
Tower of London
Museum of Mankind
Science Museum
Natural History Museum
National Maritime Museum
Thorpe Park
Chessington World of Adventures
Dickens Centre
Chartwell
Leeds Castle
Birdworld & Underwater World
Howletts Zoo Park
Hever Castle & Gardens
Penshurst Place
Kent & East Sussex Railway
Bluebell Railway
Bentley Wildfowl & Motor Museum
Drusillas Zoo Park
Brighton Aquarium & Dolphinarium
Royal Pavilion
The Living World

LONDON

It would take an entire book to do justice to London. There are countless attractions for all ages, from the big galleries and museums to the simple pleasures of riding on the top of a double-decker bus or feeding the pigeons in Trafalgar Square. Given my limitations of space, I've just selected the ten sights that in my view families of all ages will find of most interest.

The London Tourist Board (26 Grosvenor Gardens, London SW1W 0DU) publish a very useful series of guide books, the most successful of which is *Children's London*. New attractions as well as the firm, family favourites are listed; there are separate sections on indoor and outdoor London, a chapter on children's entertainments and useful advice on touring the capital with children. There's information, too, on special discounts for children; where to eat with children (did you know that there is one American restaurant that will look after children while you go off and do the shopping and sightseeing?); where to change the baby's nappy and lots more useful information.

The book is available from bookshops, London Tourist Board Information Centres or by post from the London Tourist Board, whose address is on page 16.

Another useful and particularly entertaining booklet is *Discovering London for Children* by Margaret Pearson (Shire Publications), available at most bookshops.

BRITISH MUSEUM

Great Russell Street, WC1
Tel: 01 636 1555
(Underground: Tottenham Court Road; Goodge Street; Russell Square; Holborn)

- One of the great treasure-houses of the world
- Egyptian mummies; the Elgin marbles; the Rosetta stone
- Daily life in ancient Egypt, Greece and Rome
- Oriental animal sculptures
- Clocks through the ages . . . and lots more

Cafeteria; & *(wheelchairs available – please notify)*

Open: Mon–Sat, 10–5; Sun, 2.30–6

Admission: free

LONDON PLANETARIUM

Marylebone Road, NW1
Tel: 01 486 1121
(Underground: Baker Street)

- Man-made universe in which you can study the stars, planets and comets
- Regular presentations throughout the day
- Astronomy exhibition
- 'Laserium Light' concerts, with rock and pop music

Snack bar

Open: daily, 11–4.30

Admission: Adult £2.50; Child £1.60. Combined ticket with Madame Tussaud's: Adult £5.60; Child £3.40

LONDON ZOO

Regent's Park, NW1
Tel: 01 722 3333
(Underground: Camden Town; Baker Street; then bus 74; summer only Bus Z1 from Oxford Circus or Baker Street to Zoo)

- A huge variety of mammals, birds, reptiles, fish and insects
- Chia-Chia, the rare giant panda
- Ape and monkey pavilion; elephant and rhino pavilion
- Walk-through aviary with over 140 birds
- Children's zoo farm
- Children's animal rides in summer
- 'Meet the animals' shows in summer

Pushchairs for hire; mother and baby room; large cafeteria, restaurant and cafés; indoor and outdoor picnic areas; &

Open: daily (except 25 Dec); 9–6 (summer); 10–4 (winter)

Admission: Adult £3.90; Child (5–16) £2.20; under-fives free

MADAME TUSSAUD'S

Marylebone Road, NW1
Tel: 01 935 6861
(Underground: Baker Street)

- Famous collection of wax figures
- Characters from history, films, pop, sports, etc.
- 'Chamber of Horrors' with murderers and hangmen
- Tableau of the Battle of Trafalgar, with light and sound effects

Gift shop; snack bars; & not at busy periods, please notify

Open: Mon–Fri, 10–5.30; Sat, Sun and Bank Hols, 9.30–5.30

Admission: Adult £4.40; Child £2.80. Combined ticket with Planetarium next door: Adult £5.60; Child £3.40

MUSEUM OF LONDON

London Wall, EC2
Tel: 01 600 3699
(Underground: St Paul's; Moorgate; (Mon–Fri only) Barbican)

- History of London from pre-historic times
- Models and room reconstructions from every period
- 18th-century prison cells
- Model of the Great Fire of London with light and sound effects
- Children's quizzes; excellent school holiday activities

Coffee shop; benches outside for picnics; &

Open: Tues–Sat, 10–6; Sun, 2–6

Admission: free

MUSEUM OF MANKIND

Burlington Gardens, W1
Tel: 01 437 2224
(Underground: Piccadilly Circus; Green Park)

- Life and culture of people from many lands
- Lots of activities that children can participate in
- Work sheets available; film shows Tues–Fri
- Special events during school holidays

Information Desk; &

Open: Mon–Sat, 10–5; Sun, 2.30–6

Admission: free

NATIONAL MARITIME MUSEUM

Romney Road, Greenwich, SE10
Tel: 01 858 4422 ext. 221
(Boats from Westminster, Charing Cross, Tower and Festival Piers)

- History of Britain and the sea, at peace and at war
- Nelson's Trafalgar uniform; royal state barges
- Ship models and naval weapons
- Climb aboard a paddle steamer
- Old Royal Observatory, the Greenwich Planetarium, the Cutty Sark and the Gipsy Moth are all close-by

Restaurant; picnic areas; & phone in advance

Open: Mon–Sat, 10–6 (5 in winter); Sun, 2–6 (5 in winter)

Admission: ring for prices

NATURAL HISTORY MUSEUM

Cromwell Road, SW7
Tel: 01 589 6323
(Underground: South Kensington)

- National collections of living and fossil plants and animals, rocks, minerals and meteorites
- Various exhibitions including 'Dinosaurs and their living relatives'; 'Discovering mammals' (with a 90-foot model of a blue whale), and 'Birds' (with a dodo from Mauritius)
- Family Centre, open during Easter and summer holidays

Snack bars and cafeteria; Information Desk; & please notify in advance

Open: Mon–Sat, 10–6; Sun, 1–6

Admission: Adult £2; Child £1 (Free admission 4.30–6, Mon–Fri except Bank Holidays)

SCIENCE MUSEUM

Exhibition Road, SW7
Tel: 01 589 3456
(Underground: South Kensington)

- History of science and industry
- Machines and models operated by push buttons
- Famous locomotives; old carriages; cars and aircraft
- 'Launch Pad', a gallery for children of activities demonstrating principles of physics

Cafeteria; & please telephone in advance

Open: Mon–Sat, 10–6; Sun, 2.30–6

Admission: free

TOWER OF LONDON

Tower Hill, EC3
Tel: 01 709 0765
(Underground: Tower Hill)

- The Crown Jewels
- Largest collection of early weapons and armour in Britain
- Traitors' Gate; the Tower ravens; Royal Fusiliers Museum

Souvenir shop; cafeteria; snack bar; indoor and outdoor picnic areas; & grounds only

Open: *Mar–Oct:* Mon–Sat, 9.30–5.45 (last admission 5); Sun 2–5.45 (last admission 5) *Nov–Feb:* Mon–Sat, 9.30–4.30 (last admission 4); Sun closed; Jewel House closed in Feb for annual cleaning of Crown Jewels

Admission: Adult £4.50; Child £2; over-fifteens in full-time education £3; OAPs £3

EAST SUSSEX

BRIGHTON AQUARIUM AND DOLPHINARIUM

Tel: 0273 604233/4
(seafront, Brighton)

- Dolphin displays, with seating for over 1,000 people
- 40 large tanks with fish, sea-lions, seals, turtles, etc.
- Super-X aeroplane simulator

Cafeteria

Open: all year, daily; Jan–Mar and Oct–Dec, 10–5; Apr–Sep, 10–6; last admission 45 mins before closure Closed Christmas Day

Admission: Adult £2.70; Child £1.80; OAP £2

The National Maritime Museum, Greenwich (page 20)

ROYAL PAVILION, BRIGHTON

Old Steine, Brighton
Tel: 0273 603005

- Fantastic oriental palace, created by John Nash for the Prince Regent
- Chinese-style interiors

Tea rooms

Open: all year, daily except Christmas; Jan–May and Oct–Dec, 10–5; Jun–Sep, 10–6

Admission: Adult £2; Child £1; OAP £1.25

BENTLEY WILDFOWL AND MOTOR MUSEUM

Halland
Tel: 082584 573
(7m NE of Lewes)

- Wildfowl reserve, with lakes, gardens and over 100 species of birds including swans, geese and flamingos
- Bentley House, with antiques and wildfowl paintings
- Museum of Edwardian and other vintage cars
- Miniature steam railway on summer Sundays
- Woodland walk

Gift shop; tea room; picnic site; &

Open: Apr–Oct, daily, 10.30–4.30
(5.00 Jul and Aug); Jul–Aug, Nov,
Dec, Feb, Mar, weekends,
10.30–4.30

Admission: Adult £2.50; Child
£1.20; OAP £1.50

THE BLUEBELL RAILWAY

**Sheffield Park Station, near
Uckfield
Tel: 082572 2370**
(9m N of Lewes on A275)

- 5 miles of standard-gauge track to
  Horsted Keynes
- Large collection of locomotives
  and carriages, 1865–1958
- Bluebell Cutter restaurant train
  running at weekends

*Refreshment car and shop at Sheffield
Park; bookstall and bar at Horsted
Keynes;* &

Open: Dec–Feb, Sun; Mar, Apr,
Nov, Sat and Sun; May and Oct, Sat,
Sun and Wed; Jun–Sep, daily
Open Easter Week; Santa Specials in
Dec
Contact railway for train timetable

Fares: Adult £3; Child £1.50

DRUSILLAS ZOO PARK

**Alfriston
Tel: 0323 870234**
(off A27 between Brighton and
Eastbourne)

- Excellent small zoo, with
  monkeys, penguins, llamas, etc.
- Tropical butterfly house
- Miniature railway, farmyard and
  adventure playgrounds
- Cottage bakery selling home-
  made bread, biscuits, etc.

Restaurant; pub; snacks; picnic area; &

Open: all year; end Mar–end Oct,
10.30–5.30 (all attractions open);
winter, Sat and Sun, 10.30–5.30 (zoo
only)

Admission: Adult (zoo and train)
£2.50; Child (zoo, train and
adventure playground) £2.50; OAP
(zoo and train) £1.75

THE LIVING WORLD

**Seven Sisters Country Park,
Exceat, Seaford
Tel: 0323 870100**
(by the A259, 5m W of Eastbourne)

- Fascinating living displays of
  native and foreign insects and
  other creatures
- Wide variety, from bees and
  butterflies to scorpions and hairy
  tarantulas
- Forest, river and downland walks

Showroom; gift shop; &

Open: Easter–Oct, daily, 10–5;
winter same hours, Sat, Sun and
school hols only

Admission: Adult £1.60;
Child/OAP £1 (less in winter)

KENT

KENT AND EAST SUSSEX RAILWAY

Town Station, Tenterden
Tel: 05806 5155

- 10-mile round trips on steam locomotives
- Rolling stock on view at Tenterden and Rolvenden
- 'Wine and Dine' Specials on Saturday evenings

Railway shop; picnic areas; buffet at Tenterden Station; & specially-equipped carriage for the disabled

Open: Good Fri–3rd May, weekends; 1 Jun–15 Jul, Tue, Wed, Thur, Sat, Sun; 16 Jun–4 Sep, daily; 5 Sep–13 Dec, weekends & last week Sep; 'Santa Specials' in Dec; Contact railway for exact train timetable

Fares: Adult £2.60; Child £1.30; OAP £2

CHARTWELL

Tel: 0732 866368
(2m S of Westerham)

- Home of Sir Winston Churchill
- Rooms still much as he left them: study, family dining room, several museum rooms and more
- Gardens with lakes and black swans; Golden Rose Walk; garden studio

National Trust Shop; restaurant and cafeteria; &

Open: *Mar and Nov* Sat, Sun and Wed, 11–4; *Apr–Oct* Tue–Thu, 12–5; Sat, Sun, Bank Hol Mon, 11–5 Closed Good Fri and Tue following Bank Hol Mon *Garden and Studio:* Apr–Oct, times as above

Admission: *House and Garden* Adult £2.70; Child £1.40; *Garden only* Adult £1.10; Child 60p; *Studio* 40p extra

DICKENS CENTRE

Eastgate House, High Street, Rochester
Tel: 0634 44176

- Unique, walk-through experience of Dickensian England
- Late-16th-century building, with talking tableaux and life-size models (including Scrooge, Marley's ghost, Oliver, etc.)
- Details of Dickens' life and times

Gift shop

Open: daily, except Christmas and New Year, 10–12.30, 2–5

Admission: Adult £1.40; Child/OAP 80p

HEVER CASTLE AND GARDENS

Hever, near Edenbridge
Tel: 0732 865224

- Delightful moated castle, built in 13th and 15th centuries
- Tudor-style village annexe, added in the 20th-century
- Regimental museum and exhibition on Henry VIII and Anne Boleyn (who lived here as a child)
- Magnificent grounds, with large lake, loggia, piazza, topiary

Gift shop; self-service cafeteria; &

Open: 29 Mar–6 Nov, daily
(excluding 16 Jun), 12–6 (last
admission 5) *Gardens:* 11–6

Admission: Adult £3.40; Child
£1.70; *Gardens only:* Adult £2.20;
Child £1.30

HOWLETTS ZOO PARK

Bekesbourne, near Canterbury
Tel: 0227 721286
(just off A2 between Canterbury and
Dover)

- John Aspinall's collection of
  animals, in mature parkland
- One of the largest collections of
  tigers in the world
- Largest breeding colony of gorillas
  outside America
- Baby African elephants which
  were born here

Cafeteria and refreshment kiosks

Open: all year (except Christmas
Day); 10–5 (10–4 in winter)

Admission: Adult £3.50; Child
(4–14) and OAP £2.50

LEEDS CASTLE

Maidstone
Tel: 0622 65400
(5m E of Maidstone)

- Spectacular mediaeval castle, built
  on islands in a lake
- Favourite home of the mediaeval
  queens of England
- Collection of art, furniture and
  tapestries
- Parkland with gardens; 'duckery';
  aviaries; small vineyard
- Dog Collar Museum in the
  Castle's Gatehouse

- Open-air concerts and other
  events throughout the year

Gift and plant shops; licensed restaurant;
self-service café; cream teas; barbecues; &

Open: *Castle* Jan–Mar, Sat and Sun
12–4; Apr–Oct, daily 11–5; *Grounds*
open all year, Jan–Mar and Dec, Sat
and Sun 12–4; Apr–Oct, daily 11–5

Admission: *Castle and grounds* Adult
£4.20; Child (5–15) £4; OAP £3.60
Grounds only £1 reduction on above
prices

PENSHURST PLACE

Tel: 0892 870307
(at Penshurst, 6m SW of Tonbridge)

- One of England's great mediaeval
  manor houses
- Huge Gothic Baron's Hall and fine
  state rooms
- Toy museum; venture playground;
  Tudor garden
- Park with lake, and nature trail

Gift shop; &*; self-service restaurant*

Open: Apr–early Oct, Tue–Sun and
Bank Hol Mon *Gardens* 12.30–6
House and toy museum 1–5.30

Admission: Adult £2.75; Child
£1.50; OAP £2 *Gardens only:* Adult
£2; Child £1; OAP £1.50

SURREY

BIRDWORLD AND UNDERWATERWORLD

Holt Pound
Tel: 0420 22140
(A325, 3m SW of Farnham)

- Over 1,000 birds, in 17 acres of garden and parkland
- Penguin island, bird safari ride and 'seashore walk'
- Aquarium with freshwater and marine fish
- Children's play area

Picnic area; safari shop; cafeteria; ice cream parlour; snack bar

Open: all year, daily; Apr–Aug 9.30–6, Sep 9.30–5.30, rest of year, 9.30–3.30

Admission: *Birdworld* Adult £1.90; Child £1.10 *Underwaterworld* Adult 60p; Child 35p

CHESSINGTON WORLD OF ADVENTURES

Leatherhead Road, Chessington
Tel: 037 27 27227
(on A243, 2m from the A3 and from Junction 9 of M25)

- Theme park packed with entertainment for all ages
- Western town, featuring fast rides on the Runaway Mine Train
- The Mystic East's oriental landscape with Dragon River Ride
- 'White-knuckle' rides; fantasy rides; Circus World
- Market Square; Norman castle; mill ponds etc.

- Zoo with Safari Skyway Monorail running through
- Lion and tiger enclosures; ape houses; polar bear pool
- Children's zoo

Full range of catering facilities; picnic areas; picnic tent; shops; Mother-and-baby room; &

Open: 26 Mar–30 Oct, 10–5 (all attractions); rest of the year, 10–4 (zoo only); closed Christmas Day

Admission: Adult £6.25; Child/OAP £5.25 (heavy reductions in winter)

THORPE PARK

Staines Road, Chertsey
Tel: 0932 562633
(on A320 between Staines and Chertsey)

- 500 acres of lakes and parkland with water-based theme
- Thrill rides; family rides; lots of other family activities
- Exhibits include Treasure Island, with pirate rides
- Land trains and waterbuses for transport; also boats for hire
- Cinema 180; adventure playground
- Water-skiing or windsurfing at extra cost

Restaurants; bars; ice cream parlour and kiosks

Open: 2 weeks at Easter, 10–6; weekends and Bank Hol Mon till end May, 10–6; daily till 11 September 10–6 (10–8 July and Aug); last 2 weekends in September, 10–6

Admission: Adult £6, Children £5.50, OAP £5.50

SOUTH OF ENGLAND

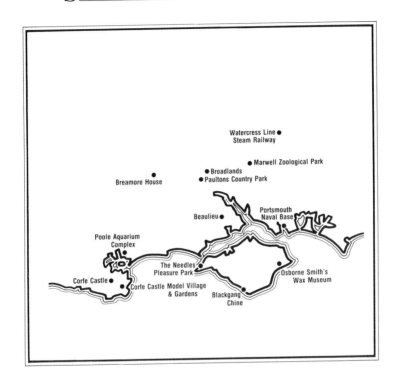

Watercress Line ●
Steam Railway

● Marwell Zoological Park

● Broadlands
● Paultons Country Park

● Breamore House

Portsmouth
Naval Base

Beaulieu ●

Poole Aquarium
Complex

The Needles
Pleasure Park

Corfe Castle ●
● Corfe Castle Model Village
   & Gardens

Blackgang
Chine

Osborne Smith's
Wax Museum

EAST DORSET

CORFE CASTLE

Tel: 0929 480442
(5m NW of Swanage, on A351
Wareham to Swanage road)

- Splendid castle ruins on hill,
  overlooking picturesque village

Tea room

Open: Nov–end-Feb, weekends
only 12–4; Mar–end-Oct, daily 10–6

Admission: Adult £1.50; Child 75p

CORFE CASTLE MODEL VILLAGE AND GARDENS

**The Square, Corfe Castle
Tel: 0929 480091**

- Castle, village and church lovingly
  recreated
- Delightful old-English gardens

Cafeteria; &

Open: Easter–end-Sep, daily, 10–6;
Oct, Sun–Thur, 11–4

Admission: Adult 70p; Child/OAP
35p; Under-fives free

HAMPSHIRE

BEAULIEU

Tel: 0590 612345
(on B3056 between Southampton and Lyndhurst)

- Palace House (Lord Montagu's ancestral home) and gardens
- Beaulieu Abbey and exhibition of monastic life
- National Motor Museum, with 250 vehicles, from 1894
- Monorail; veteran bus rides; model railway
- 'Transporama' sound-and-vision presentation
- 'Wheels': mobile pods taking you through 100 years of futuristic motoring
- Regular events, e.g. car rallies; craft fairs

Shops; cafeteria; Mother-and-baby room; & limited

Open: all year except Christmas Day; Easter–Oct, 10–6; Nov–Easter, 10–5

Admission: Adult £4.75; Child £3.25; OAP £3.75 (extra costs for some attractions)

BREAMORE HOUSE

Fordingbridge
Tel: 0725 22468
(8m S of Salisbury, off A338)

- Impressive Elizabethan manor house
- Fine collection of furniture and paintings
- Carriage Museum in the Queen Anne stables
- Countryside Museum, showing development of village life

- Annual events, such as agricultural, steam engines, craft fairs

Cafeteria; & except 1st floor of house

Open: 2–5.30; *April* Tue, Wed, Sun & Easter *May, Jun, Sep* Tue, Wed, Thur, Sat, Sun and Bank Holidays *Aug* daily

Admission: Adult £2.80; Child £1.40; OAP £2.30

BROADLANDS

Romsey
Tel: 0794 516878
(entrance on A31 at Romsey)

- Beautiful eighteenth-century house, the former home of Lord Mountbatten
- Selection from the Imperial Crown Jewels (including the Queen's wedding tiara) and Prince of Wales' investiture crown
- Mountbatten Exhibition and audio-visual show

Tea rooms; picnic area; 2 gift shops; self-service restaurant

Open: Apr–Sep, 10–5; closed Mon except Aug, Sep and Bank Hols

Admission: Adult £3.20; Child (12–16) £1.80; OAP £2.40

MARWELL ZOOLOGICAL PARK

Colden Common, Winchester
Tel: 096274 406
(6m S of Winchester on the B2177)

- 100 acres of beautiful park, with giraffes, camels, rhinos, antelope, monkeys and many more animals, including some rare species
- One of the largest collections of big cats in Britain
- Free guided tours in summer, and wildlife lectures
- Exhibition
- Children's amusements and playground

Cafeteria; refreshment kiosks; gift shops; picnic areas; &

Open: daily (except Christmas Day) 10–6 (or dusk)

Admission: Adult £3.20; Child £2; OAP £2.70

MID-HANTS RAILWAY plc 'WATERCRESS LINE'

Alresford Station, Alresford
Tel: 096273 3810/4200
(7m E of Winchester, off the A31)

- Steam trains running over 10 miles between Alresford and Alton through lovely countryside and the famous watercress beds
- 'Wine and Dine' train, fortnightly on Saturday evenings

Souvenir shops at Alresford, Ropley, Alton; bar/buffet car facilities on all trains

Open: end Mar–end Oct, weekends and Bank Hols; Jul–Aug daily; Santa Steam specials during Dec weekends. Trains from late morning

Fares: *Rover Ticket* (go as you please) Adult £4; Child £2; OAP £2.60; cheaper rates for single journeys

PAULTONS COUNTRY PARK

Ower
Tel: 0703 814442
(on the A36/A31; M27 exit 2)

- Over 1000 exotic birds and animals
- Large gardens and 10-acre lake with waterfowl
- Village Life Museum; Romany Museum; working watermill
- Kids' Kingdom, with giant slides and cableways
- Captain Blood's Caverns (haunted house)
- Magic Forest, with favourite nursery rhyme figures coming to life
- Rides on Rio Grande train around park
- Japanese Garden; Land of the Dinosaurs; Rabbit Ride

2 self-service restaurants; burger bars; refreshments; shops; picnic areas; nursing room; gift garden and tuck shops; &

Open: daily, 12 Mar–30 Oct, 10–6.30 (last admission 4.30); earlier closing spring and autumn

Admission: Adult £3.00; Child/ OAP £2.50

POOLE AQUARIUM COMPLEX

The Quay, Poole
Tel: 0202 686712

- 42 tanks in historic quayside warehouse
- Oceanic shark; piranhas; giant turtles
- Serpentarium, with lizards, crocodiles, pythons, toads, etc.
- Insect collection, with tarantulas and scorpions
- Model museum; model railway

Open: daily (except 24/25 Dec) 10–9 in summer; 10.30–4.30 (weekdays), 10–5.30 (weekends) in winter

Admission: Adult £1.80; Students/OAPs £1.50; Child 90p

PORTSMOUTH NAVAL BASE

Tel: 0705 822351 (museum) 0705 750521 (Mary Rose) 0705 819604 (HMS Victory) 0705 291379 (HMS Warrior)

- HMS Victory – Nelson's flagship at Trafalgar
- The Mary Rose – Henry VIII's famous flagship – and contents
- HMS Warrior, Britain's first iron-hulled battleship
- Naval Museum

Catering facilities

Open: daily, except Christmas Day

Admission: *HMS Victory* Adult £1.50 and £1.80 (high season); Child/OAP 90p and £1; *Mary Rose* Adult £2.50/£2.80; Child/OAP £1.50/£1.80; *HMS Warrior* Adult £3; Child £1.50; *Naval Museum* Adult 50p, Child/OAP 25p; Family Ticket £1.25

ISLE OF WIGHT

BLACKGANG CHINE

Chale, near Ventnor
Tel: 0983 730330

- 20-acre fantasy theme park, with gardens on cliff tops
- Smuggler Land; Crooked House; Maze; Dinosaurs
- Water Gardens; Jungle Land; Maritime Exhibition and lots more

Cafés and bars

Open: daily 10–5 in Apr, May and Oct; daily 10–10 in Jun, Jul, Aug, Sep

Admission: (all-in ticket) Adult £2.75; Child £1.75

THE NEEDLES PLEASURE PARK

Alum Bay, Totland Bay
Tel: 0983 752401

- Large pleasure park, with lots to see and do
- Breathtaking ride on chairlift to beach with views of coloured cliffs, Needles rocks and lighthouse
- Boat trips; model railway; glass-blowing centre; crafts; pottery
- Amusements centre

Shops; bar; cafeteria

Open: Feb–Oct inclusive, 10–5 approximately

Admission: no admission charge; charges for individual attractions

The National Motor Museum, Beaulieu (page 28)

OSBORNE-SMITH'S WAX MUSEUM

High Street, Brading
Tel: 0983 407286

- Renowned museum set in the Ancient Rectory Mansion
- Chamber of Horrors set in the Castle Dungeons
- Wax figures; period furniture
- Clever sound, light and motion effects

Open: all year, daily including Christmas Day; summer, 10–10; Oct–Apr; 10–5

Admission: Adult £1.75; Child under 14 £1.25; under-threes free, *Bargain combined ticket* (to visit Wax Museum and Osborne-Smith's Animal World, next door) Adult £2.75; Child £1.90

WEST COUNTRY

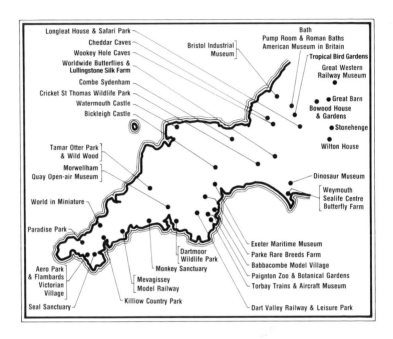

Longleat House & Safari Park
Cheddar Caves
Wookey Hole Caves
Worldwide Butterflies & Lullingstone Silk Farm
Combe Sydenham
Cricket St Thomas Wildlife Park
Watermouth Castle
Bickleigh Castle

Bristol Industrial Museum

Bath
Pump Room & Roman Baths
American Museum in Britain
Tropical Bird Gardens
Great Western Railway Museum
Great Barn
Bowood House & Gardens
Stonehenge
Wilton House

Tamar Otter Park & Wild Wood
Morwellham Quay Open-air Museum

World in Miniature

Paradise Park

Aero Park & Flambards Victorian Village
Seal Sanctuary

Mevagissey Model Railway
Killiow Country Park

Dartmoor Wildlife Park
Monkey Sanctuary

Dinosaur Museum
Weymouth Sealife Centre Butterfly Farm

Exeter Maritime Museum
Parke Rare Breeds Farm
Babbacombe Model Village
Paignton Zoo & Botanical Gardens
Torbay Trains & Aircraft Museum
Dart Valley Railway & Leisure Park

AVON

AMERICAN MUSEUM IN BRITAIN

Claverton Manor, near Bath
Tel: 0225 60503

- 18 rooms showing 17th–19th-century domestic American life
- Sections devoted to American Indians, Opening of the West, etc.
- Folk-art gallery; American gardens

Open: Easter–Oct; Tue–Sun and Bank Holidays

Admission: Adult £3; Child (under 14) £2; OAP £2.50; *grounds only:* £1

BATH PUMP ROOM AND ROMAN BATHS

Stall Street, Bath
Tel: 0225 61111

- Elegant Georgian room, once the social centre of Bath
- Remains of the famous Roman baths
- Drink spa water overlooking the hot springs

&

Open: all year, daily, 9.30–6 (10–6 on Sun)

Admission: Adult £2, Child £1.15

BRISTOL INDUSTRIAL MUSEUM

Prince's Wharf, Bristol
Tel: 0272 299771

- Docklands museum displaying 300 years of industrial regional history
- Water, air and land vehicles
- Fairbairn steam crane
- 1930s steam locomotive working on some weekends

&

Open: all year, Sat–Wed, 10–1, 2–3

Admission: free

CORNWALL

CORNWALL AERO PARK AND FLAMBARDS VICTORIAN VILLAGE

Helston, off A3083
Tel: 0326 574549

- Award-winning, life-size Victorian village
- Fully stocked shops; carriages; fashions
- Britain in the Blitz exhibition
- Aero Park with historic aircraft
- Self-drive, space hyperglide rangers (jeeps)
- Video games; boating lake; radio-controlled boats, etc.
- Garden centre
- Children's play areas

Cafeteria and garden refreshments; picnic area

Open: Easter–Oct, daily, 10–dusk (last admission 5); July–Aug, 10–9.30

Admission: Adult £3.30; Child £1.50; OAP £2.60

KILLIOW COUNTRY PARK

Kea
Tel: 0872 72768
(3m S of Truro on A39)

- Beautiful, landscaped parkland, with rare breeds sanctuary, coaching and carriage centre, farm museum
- Working pottery, spinning and weaving display
- Carriage rides
- Pets' corner and adventure play area
- Golf course and driving range

Old Kitchen Coffee Shop; picnic areas; &

Open: Apr–Sep, every day; golf course and driving range open all year (separate charge)

Admission: Adult £1; Child 50p

MEVAGISSEY MODEL RAILWAY

Meadow Street, Mevagissey
Tel: 0726 842457

- Over 2,000 trains from many countries
- Nearly 50 trains automatically programmed
- Exquisite layout of landscapes and buildings

Model shop; &

Open: Easter hols; spring Bank Holiday–Oct every day from 11; Nov–May: Sun pm only

Admission: Adult £1.20; Child/OAP 80p

THE MONKEY SANCTUARY

Tel: 05036 2532
(3m E of Looe)

- Protected breeding colony of woolly monkeys
- Donkeys, rabbits and other animals

Light refreshments; &

Open: Easter and May–Sep, Sun–Thur, 10.30–5.30

Admission: Adult £2.50; Child £1

PARADISE PARK

Hayle
Tel: 0736 753365

- Outstanding collection of rare and endangered birds
- Rare breeds of animals, plus young ones for children to touch
- Miniature railway; amusement centre

&; *cafe and shop (summer only)*

Open: all year, every day

Admission: Adult £2.50; Child £1.50; OAP £2.00

SEAL SANCTUARY

Gweek
Tel: 032622 361
(4m E of Helston)

- Haven for seals that are washed up around the Cornish coast
- Woodlands and woodland walks

Open: all year, every day (except Christmas Day), 9.30–5.30/6

Admission: Adult £2.00; Child £1 (3–16)

TAMAR OTTER PARK AND WILD WOOD

Navarino, North Petherwin, near Launceston
Tel: 056685 646

- Recently opened park (1986) devoted to conservation of otters and other wild life
- Otters in large, open, natural enclosures
- Lake; water-fowl, aviaries
- Nature trail and adventure playground

&; *tea room; gift shop*

Open: May–Oct, 10.30–6

Admission: Adult £2; Child £1; OAP £1.60

WORLD IN MINIATURE

Goonhavern, near Perranporth
Tel: 087257 2828

- Large-scale models of the world's famous statues and buildings (e.g. Statue of Liberty, Buckingham Palace)
- 12 acres of beautiful landscaped gardens
- Life-size reconstruction of a street in Tombstone, a Wild West town
- Live circus, Cinema 180

Large cafeteria; large gift shop; &

Open: Mar–Oct, every day

Admission: Adult £2.95; Child £1.80

DEVON

BABBACOMBE MODEL VILLAGE

**Babbacombe, Torquay
Tel: 0803 38669**

- Model English countryside, with town, villages, farms, pubs, etc.
- Set in 4 acres of beautiful gardens

&

Open: all-year, daily, summer 9–10, winter 10–4

Admission: Adult £2; Child £1

BICKLEIGH CASTLE

Tel: 08845 363
(4m S of Tiverton on A396)

- Eleventh-century chapel: the oldest complete building in Devon
- Armoury; Guard Room; Great Hall; Stuart-period farmhouse
- Moated gardens and good views from tower
- 'Mary Rose' exhibition and display of World War II prisoner escape equipment

Shops; tea room/refreshments in thatched barn; &

Open: 2–5, Easter week, Wed, Sun and Bank Holidays to spring Bank Holiday, then every day till early Oct except Sat

Admission: Adult £2; Child (5–16) £1

DARTMOOR WILDLIFE PARK

**Sparkwell
Tel: 075537 209**
(7m E of Plymouth, off A38)

- Over 100 species of animals and birds, from lions, tigers and wolves to seals and water-fowl
- Falconry displays Easter– September

Restaurant; shop; &

Open: all year, daily, 10–dusk

Admission: Adult £3.20; Child £2

DART VALLEY STEAM RAILWAY AND LEISURE PARK

**Buckfastleigh, off A38
Tel: 0364 42338**

- 7-mile steam train rides from Buckfastleigh to Totnes and back
- Beautiful Dart Valley scenery
- Museum; rolling stock and viewing areas at Buckfastleigh

Shop; restaurant; picnic spots at Buckfastleigh; &

Open: Easter–May Bank Holidays, Jun–Sep, daily

Admission: (includes entrance to museum) Adult £3.80 return; Child £2.60 return

EXETER MARITIME MUSEUM

The Quay, Exeter
Tel: 0392 58075

- Over 100 boats from all over the world
- Brunel's steam dredger; Arab dhow; Hong Kong Junk
- Indoor exhibits in nineteenth-century warehouses
- Ferry to the boats and boats to hire

Tea rooms; gift shop

Open: all year, daily (except Christmas and Boxing Days)

Admission: Adult £2.80; Child £1.50; OAP £2.50; *Family Ticket* £7.50

MORWELLHAM QUAY OPEN-AIR MUSEUM

Tel: 0822 832766
(off A390 between Tavistock and Gunnislake)

- Recreated Victorian copper port, in unspoilt countryside
- Tramway that takes you down into an ancient coppermine
- Craftsmen dressed in period costume
- Victorian farm with animals and two 19th-century cottages
- Carriage rides drawn by shire horses

Restaurant; shops (summer only)

Open: all year, daily apart from Christmas week

Admission: Adult £4.15; Child £2.85; OAP £3.45

PAIGNTON ZOO AND BOTANICAL GARDENS

Tel: 0803 527936
(½m from town centre on Totnes Road)

- Third biggest zoo in Britain
- 75 acres of exotic plants and trees, lakes and streams
- The Ark family activity-centre
- Miniature train; nature trail

Self-service restaurants; bar; shops; &

Open: all year, daily except Christmas Day

Admission: Adult £2.90; Child £1.90

PARKE RARE BREEDS FARM

Bovey Tracey
Tel: 0626 833909

- Rare and indigenous breeds of farm animals and fowl
- Beautiful parkland setting
- Paddock and display areas
- Pets' corner
- China model-pig collection

Craft shop; information centre; café

Open: Apr–Oct, daily, 10–6, last admission 5

Admission: Adult £2; Child (3–14) £1.20; OAP £1.60

TORBAY TRAINS AND AIRCRAFT MUSEUM

High Blagdon, Paignton
Tel: 0803 553540

- Torbay Aircraft Museum
- Torbay indoor model railway (one of largest in the country)

- Devonshire collection of period costume, from mid-18th century
- Kenneth More Gardens
- Video theatres, with relevant films and documentaries on aircraft

Souvenir shop; cafeteria; picnic area; &

Open: 30 Mar–25 Sep; low season 10–5, high season 10–6

Admission: Adult £2.50; Child under 16 £1.50; OAP £2

WATERMOUTH CASTLE

Berrynarbor, near Ilfracombe
Tel: 0271 63879
(on the coast between Ilfracombe and Combe Martin)

- Castle with lots of family entertainment from mechanical music demonstrations to model railway and cycle museum
- Great Granny's kitchens; smugglers' dungeon
- Domestic dairy and cider-making exhibits
- Gardens, aviaries and pets' corner
- Children's play area

Tea room; picnic area; & *partial access*

Open: 3 Apr–19 May, Sun–Thur from 2.30; 22 May–26 June, Mon–Fri from 11 (Sun 2); 27 Jun–4 Sep, Mon–Fri from 10 (Sun 11); 5 Sep–30 Sep, Mon–Fri from 11 (Sun 2) Last admission 4pm; never open Saturdays

Admission: Adult £3.60; Child £2.60; OAP £3.10

SOMERSET

CHEDDAR CAVES

Tel: 0934 742343

- Show caves with stalagtites and stalagmites at foot of Cheddar Gorge
- Fantasy grotto with Hologram exhibition
- Museum with 10,000-year-old Cheddar man on display
- 'Jacob's ladder', with over 300 steps to top of the gorge

Open: all year, daily except Christmas Day and Boxing Day

Admission: *all-in ticket* Adult £2.95; Child £1.60. *Gough's cave only* Adult £1.70; Child 85p

COMBE SYNDENHAM

Monksilver, near Taunton
Tel: 0984 56284

- Elizabethan hall; home of Sir Francis Drake's wife
- Legends, paintings, furnishings
- Gardens with deer park, birds of prey, trout ponds
- Woodland walks around the estate

Tea room; gift shop

Open: Apr–Oct, Mon–Fri

Admission: *house, garden and country park* Adult £2.20; Child £1.50; OAP £1.80; *country park only* Adult £1.80; Child £1.50

Dart Valley Steam Railway (page 35)

CRICKET ST THOMAS WILDLIFE PARK

Tel: 046030 755
(on A30 between Chard and Crewkerne)

- Film location for BBC's 'To the Manor Born'
- Wild animals and birds, including elephants, monkeys, sea-lions, penguins
- Country life museum, with crafts and workshops
- Woodland railway; playground; pets' corner
- Walk-through tropical aviary

Picnic area; licensed restaurant; garden shop; craft shop; &

Open: all year, daily, 10–3.30 (winter, shops closed), 10–6 (summer)

Admission: Adult £3.50; Child (3–14) £2.50; OAP £3

TROPICAL BIRD GARDENS

Rode
Tel: 0373 830326
(10m S of Bath)

- Hundreds of richly coloured exotic birds, in beautiful setting
- 17 acres of woodland, flower gardens and ornamental lakes
- Natural history exhibition
- Pets' corner (summer only), aquarium and reptile house

Licensed cafeteria in summer

Open: all year, daily except
Christmas Day

Admission: Adult £2.30; Child
£1.20; OAP £1.90

WOOKEY HOLE CAVES

Tel: 0749 72243
(2m NW of Wells, off M5)

- Spectacular caves with stalagmites
  and stalactites
- Working Victorian papermill
- Madame Tussaud's storeroom
  with around 200 famous heads
- 'Old Penny Pier Arcade'
- Fairground by Night collection,
  with working organ
- Swimming pool open in summer

Catering facilities; shop; &

Open: all year, daily except
Christmas

Admission: Adult £3.35; Child
£2.25; OAP £2.85; *Family Ticket*
(2+2) £9.90

WEST DORSET

DINOSAUR MUSEUM

**Icen Way, Dorchester
Tel: 0305 69880**

- Only museum in Britain devoted
  entirely to dinosaurs
- Lively displays with full-size
  models; fossils; bones; footprints
- Computerised, mechanical and
  electronic displays
- Video gallery

&*; coffee shop; licensed restaurant*

Open: all year, daily (except 25/26
Dec and 1 Jan)

Admission: Adult £1.75; Child
£1.25; OAP £1.50; *Family Ticket*
(2+2) £5.50

WEYMOUTH BUTTERFLY FARM

**Lodmoor Country Park,
Weymouth
Tel: 0305 783311**
(on outskirts of town)

- Large tropical jungle set under
  glass, with monsoons and
  waterfalls
- Up to 1,000 exotic butterflies in
  flight
- Spider and insect display, with
  tarantulas, scorpions, locusts, etc.

&

Open: Easter–Oct, daily, 10–5

Admission: Adult £1.75; Child
(5–16) £1.10; *Family Ticket* £5

WEYMOUTH SEA LIFE CENTRE

**Lodmoor Country Park,
Weymouth
Tel: 0305 788 255**

- Largest display of marine life in
  Britain
- Ocean Tunnel, Cliff Walk, Island
  Walkway, touch tanks
- Future of the Seas exhibition
- Blue Whale splash pool with
  adventure play area

Coffee shop; gift shop; &

Open: Feb–Nov, daily

Admission: Adult £2.25; Child
£1.35; *Family Ticket* (2+2) 70p off

WORLDWIDE BUTTERFLIES AND LULLINGSTONE SILK FARM

Tel: 0935 74608
(On A30 between Sherborne and Yeovil)

- Tropical jungle with butterflies breeding naturally
- Silk farm with rearing and reeling of English silk
- Butterfly house and garden
- Beautiful grounds and outdoor (summer) butterfly gardens

Basic refreshments

Open: Apr–Oct, daily 10–5

Admission: Adult £2.65; Child £1.50; OAP £1.95

WILTSHIRE

BOWOOD HOUSE AND GARDENS

Tel: 0249 812102
(off A4 between Calne and Chippenham)

- Fine 18th century house with paintings and porcelain
- Landscaped park with lake, terraces, waterfalls, grottos
- 50 acres of Rhododendron Walks
- Large adventure playground

&; cafeteria; licensed restaurant; gift shop; garden centre

Open: 26 Mar–16 Oct, daily 11–6

Admission: Adult £2.70; Child £1.50; OAP £2

GREAT BARN

Avebury
Tel: 06723 555
on A361 near Marlborough

- 17th-century thatched barn, with displays of thatching, saddlery, shepherding, cheese-making and other rural crafts
- Regular programme of craft demonstrations and folk dancing

Refreshments; shop with books and crafts; &

Open: Easter–Oct, daily; Nov to Easter, Sat and Sun

Admission: Adult 90p; Child/OAP 45p; Family Ticket (2 + 2) £1.90

GREAT WESTERN RAILWAY MUSEUM

Faringdon Road, Swindon
Tel: 0793 26161 ext 3131

- Recreation of the Great Western Railway era, with historic locomotives, models, illustrations, posters, tickets, maps, photos
- No working engines

Open: all year daily, except Christmas Day and Good Friday, 10–5, Sun 2–5

Admission: Adult 90p; Child/OAP 45p

LONGLEAT HOUSE AND SAFARI PARK

Warminster
Tel: 09853 551
(signposted from Warminster)

- Splendid Elizabethan house, lived in by the Marquis of Bath
- Various art treasures, fine furniture and magnificent ceilings
- Park by Capability Brown; butterfly gardens
- Bygones and dolls' houses; VIP vehicles
- Miniature railway and 'the world's largest maze'
- Dr Who Exhibition; boat rides
- Children's adventure castle; pets' corner
- Safari Park: 7 reserves with the well-known lions, plus giraffes, monkeys, wolves, rhinos and the rare Siberian tigers

Various eating places including restaurant; cafeteria, pub; &; kiosks and shops

Open: *Longleat House* all year, daily (except Christmas Day), 10–6 (10–4 in winter) *Safari Park* 12 Mar–30 Oct, daily 10–6 (last car 5.30)

Admission: *House* Adult £2.80; Child (4–14) £1; OAP £2.30 *Safari* Adult £3.50; Child £2.50; OAP £3.00 *Discount (all-in) ticket* Adult £7; Child £5; OAP £6

STONEHENGE

enquiries to Historic Buildings & Monuments Commission
Tel: 01 734 6010
(off A344, 2m W of Amesbury)

- World-famous prehistoric monument
- Circle of giant blocks of stones, whose function remains a mystery
- Mid-summer Druid celebrations

Open: all year, daily; Sun pm only

Admission: Adult £1.30; Child 65p; OAP £1

WILTON HOUSE

Tel: 0722 743115
(on A30, 2½m W of Salisbury)

- 17th-century mansion of great beauty, with fine state rooms, furnishings and art collection
- Exhibition of 7,000 model soldiers
- 20 acres of lawns

Garden centre; self service restaurant; &

Open: 29 Mar–16 Oct, Tue–Sat inclusive and Bank Hol Mon, 11–6; Sun 1–6

Admission: *House, grounds and exhibition* Adult £3.35; Child £1.90 *House and grounds only* Adult £2.50; Child £1.25 *Grounds only* Adult £1; Child 70p

THAMES AND CHILTERNS

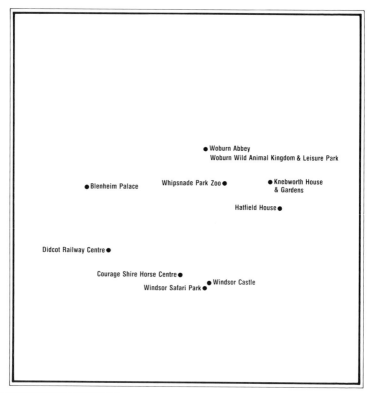

- Woburn Abbey
  Woburn Wild Animal Kingdom & Leisure Park

- Blenheim Palace   Whipsnade Park Zoo ●   ● Knebworth House
                                                 & Gardens

                                         Hatfield House ●

Didcot Railway Centre ●

Courage Shire Horse Centre ●
              Windsor Safari Park ● ● Windsor Castle

BEDFORDSHIRE

WHIPSNADE PARK ZOO

Dunstable
Tel: 0582 872171
(3m S of Dunstable)

- Over 2,000 animals, including sea-lions, tigers, bears, rhinos, rare wild horses and deer
- Performing bottle-nosed dolphins
- Narrow-gauge railway
- Children's railway

Cafeteria and refreshment kiosks; &

Open: Mon–Sat, 10–6; Sun, Bank Hol Mon 10–7 (or dusk); shut Christmas Day

Admission: Adult £3.50; Child (5–15) £1.80; OAP £1.80

WOBURN ABBEY

Tel: 0525 290666
(8m NW of Dunstable)

- Home of the Dukes of Bedford, set in 3,000-acre deer-park
- Fine collections of paintings, porcelain, silver, furniture

Antiques centre; pottery and gift shops

Open: off-season, weekends only, *park* 10.30–3.45 *abbey,* 11–4; end Mar–end Oct *park* daily 10–4.45, *abbey,* Mon–Sat 11–5, (Sun, Bank Hol Mon 11–5.30)

Admission: Adult £3.50; Child £1.50; OAP £2.75 *Family tickets £9* (2+2) or £10 (2+3)

WOBURN WILD ANIMAL KINGDOM AND LEISURE PARK

Tel: 0525 290246
(9m NW of Dunstable)

- Drive-through safari park with lions, tigers, bears, white rhino and elephants
- Passenger railway
- Carousel; helter-skelter; sea-lion shows and boating lakes

Amusement centre; picnic area; &

Open: 12 Mar–30 Oct; daily, 10–5

Admission: Adult £4.50; Child (4–14) £3.50; OAP £4

Whipsnade Park Zoo, Dunstable

43

BERKSHIRE

COURAGE SHIRE HORSE CENTRE

Tel: 062882 4848
(on A4, 2m W of Maidenhead)

- Up to 12 Courage Shire horses, plus small animals and birds
- Farrier's workshop and occasional wheelright or cooper at work
- Displays of harness and brass and hundreds of trophies
- Free guided tours throughout the day
- Audio-visual presentation

Tea room; souvenir shop; &

Open: 1 Mar–31 Oct, daily, 1–5 (last admission 4)

Admission: Adult £1.75; Child (4–15)/OAP/Disabled £1.25

WINDSOR CASTLE

Tel: 0753 868286

- Splendid State Apartments
- Queen Mary's dolls' house
- Changing exhibition of drawings from Queen's collection
- Beautiful St George's Chapel
- 'Royalty and Empire' Exhibition at the Central Station, where Madame Tussaud's have re-created a scene from Queen Victoria's 1897 Diamond Jubilee in its original surroundings; impressive theatre presentation bringing famous Victorians to life

Open: most of the year but very complex opening hours – telephone for details

Admission: *State Apartments* Adult £1.80; Child 80p *Queen Mary's doll's house and drawings exhibition* (combined ticket) Adult 80p; Child 40p *St George's chapel* Adult £1.50; Child 60p

WINDSOR SAFARI PARK

Tel: 0753 869841
(20m W of London on B3022 Windsor–Bracknell road)

- 7 drive-through reserves with lions, tigers, elephants, etc.
- Seaworld with dolphins, sea-lions and killer whale
- Birds of prey show
- Adventure playcentre
- Chimpanzee enclosure and walk-through butterfly house

Gift shop; cafeterias; bar; & *partial access*

Open: daily from 10, except Christmas

Admission: Adult £5.95; Child (4–14) £4.95; OAP £4.95

HERTFORDSHIRE

HATFIELD HOUSE

Hatfield
Tel: 07072 62823
(on A1000)

- Famous Jacobean house with magnificent gardens
- State rooms with fine paintings; furniture; tapestries; armour
- Surviving wing of the Royal Palace of Hatfield, where Elizabeth I spent much of her childhood and held her first Council of State

- Annual events including 'Living Crafts' (May), 'Festival of Gardens' (June)
- Guided tours every day except Sundays and Bank Holidays

Restaurant and cafeteria; &

Open: 25 Mar–9 Oct, Tue–Sat, 12–4.15; Sun, 2–5.30; Bank Hol Mon 11–5

Admission: *Hall, park and gardens* Adult £2.95; Child £2.15; *Park and gardens* Adult £1.70; Child £1.30

KNEBWORTH HOUSE AND GARDENS

Tel: 0438 812661
(Signposted A1(M) in southern Stevenage)

- Elaborate Tudor mansion, with fine paintings and furniture
- Exhibition on Vice-regal India
- 250 acres of parkland
- Adventure playground, nature trail and narrow-gauge railway
- Special events on certain days

Restaurant; picnic areas

Open: 26 Mar–22 May, Sat, Sun, Bank Hol Mon and school holidays; 28 May–11 Sep, Sat, Sun, Tue–Fri; 12 Sep–2 Oct, Sat, Sun; *Park* 11–5.30, *House and gardens* 12–5

Admission: *House, park and garden* Adult £3; Child/OAP £2.50 *Park, garden and playground* £1.50 per person

OXFORDSHIRE

BLENHEIM PALACE

Woodstock
Tel: 0993 811325
(8m N of Oxford on A34)

- Splendid classical mansion, birthplace of Winston Churchill and now home of the Duke of Marlborough
- Fine collection of furniture, paintings and tapestries
- Churchill exhibition
- Beautifully landscaped gardens
- Butterfly house and adventure playground
- Trips on narrow gauge railway or by boat on the lake

Park and plant centre; cafeteria and self-service restaurant; shops; picnic areas
Open: *park* daily, 9–5, *house* mid-Mar–Oct, daily, 10.30–6

Admission: Adult £4.20; Child (5–15) £2; OAP £3.10

DIDCOT RAILWAY CENTRE

Tel: 0235 817200
(10m S of Oxford, by Didcot station)

- Large collection of locomotives, coaches and rolling stock,
- Original engine shed; coaling stage; typical station
- Special Steam Days

Refreshment room; 2 dining coaches on some days; souvenir shops

Open: mid-Mar–end Dec, Sat and Sun, 11–5; Apr–end Oct; daily, 11–5

Admission: *steam days* Adult £2; Child/OAP £1.30; *Family ticket* £6 *non-steam days* Adult £1.50; Child/OAP £1, *Family ticket* £4.50

EAST ANGLIA

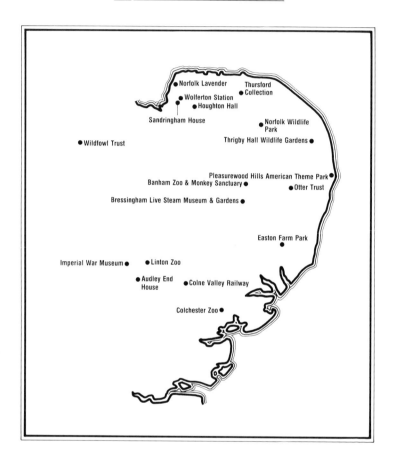

CAMBRIDGESHIRE

IMPERIAL WAR MUSEUM

Duxford
Tel: 0223 833963
(9m S of Cambridge)

- Former Battle-of-Britain fighter station

- Over 90 historic and important aircraft, including Concorde
- Hangars dating from First World War
- Flying most Sundays in summer and five special events
- Adventure playground

Restaurant; shop; picnic area; & partial access

Open: mid-March–Oct, daily, 10.30–5.30

Admission: Adult £3.50; Child/OAP £1.80

LINTON ZOO

Tel: 0223 891308
(10m SE of Cambridge along B1952, just off A604)

- Varied collection of wildlife (lions, leopards, bears, etc.) in 10½ acres of gardens
- Children's play area

Café; shop; picnic area; &

Open: daily except Christmas and Boxing Day, 10–7 or dusk

Admission: Adult £2.20; Child £1.10; OAP £1.60

WILDFOWL TRUST

Peakirk, near Peterborough
Tel: 0733 252271
(7m N of Peterborough on B1443)

- 17 acres of water-gardens, with over 100 species of duck, geese and swans, and a flock of Chilean flamingos
- Occasional indoor film shows and talks September–April

Refreshments (seasonal); shop

Open: daily except Christmas and Boxing Day, 9.30–dusk

Admission: Adult £1.70; Child 80p; OAP £1.20

ESSEX

AUDLEY END HOUSE

Saffron Walden
Tel: 0799 22399
(1m W of Saffron Walden, on B1383, M11 exits 8 and 9, northbound only)

- Palatial Jacobean house, set in a landscaped park
- Richly decorated interiors, with fine furniture and paintings
- Occasional spring and summer special events

English Heritage shop; restaurant

Open: Apr–2nd week Oct, Tue–Sun and Bank Hol Mon; *house* 1–5, *grounds* 12–6

Admission: Adult £2.50; Child £1.50; OAP £1.85

COLCHESTER ZOO

Stanway
Tel: 0206 330253
(take A604 Cambridge exit from A12)

- Over 150 species of animals, including big cats, sea-lions, rhinos
- Special events: elephants' bath time; meet the python; daily falconry displays and sea-lion shows
- Pony/donkey rides; lakeside miniature railway
- Children's pets' corner; reptile house; aquarium

Picnic areas; refreshments; &; baby-changing facilities

Open: all year (except Christmas Day), 9.30–5.30 or dusk

Admission: Adult £2.70; Child £1.30; OAP £2.10; disabled £1.10

COLNE VALLEY RAILWAY

Castle Hedingham
Tel: 0787 61174
(4m NW of Halstead on A604)

- Steam-hauled rides through pretty part of Colne Valley
- Static displays of locomotives and rolling stock

Carriage restaurant; picnic area by River Colne

Open: *Static displays* Mar–Christmas, daily except Mon, 11–5; *Steam days* Easter–Oct on most Suns, school summer holidays, Wed and Bank Hol weekends (except Christmas and New Year)

Admission: Adult £1.20; Child 60p; *Steam days* Adult £2.50; Child £1.25 (includes free rides)

NORFOLK

BANHAM ZOO AND MONKEY SANCTUARY

Tel: 095 387 476
(on B113, 6m NW of Diss)

- Over 20 acres, with camels, panthers, penguins and a large collection of rare monkeys
- Chimp house; zebra house; leopard house; reptile and insect houses
- Miniature-gauge steam railway
- Woodland walk, with monkey jungle island
- Pets' and farmyard corner

Licensed cafeteria; shops; indoor and outdoor picnic areas

Open: daily, 10–dusk

Admission: Adult £2.50; Child £1.25

BRESSINGHAM LIVE STEAM MUSEUM AND GARDENS

Tel: 0379 88 386
(3m W of Diss on A1066)

- 6 acres of beautiful gardens, with over 5,000 species of plants
- Impressive steam museum, with over 50 steam engines
- Steam-hauled train rides on 5 miles of track
- Steam-driven roundabout

Refreshments; shop; &

Open: *museum only* Easter and Sun in April *museum and gardens* Bank Hol Mon and Sun, 1 May–25 Sep; Thur from 2 Jun–8 Sep and Wed in Aug, 11–5.30

Admission: Adult £2; Child £1; OAP £1.50

HOUGHTON HALL

Tel: 048522 569
(off A148, 14m E of King's Lynn)

- Fine Palladian-style mansion, built for Sir Robert Walpole
- State rooms, with many original furnishings
- Beautiful parkland, with white fallow deer
- Stables, with heavy horses and Shetland ponies
- Collection of some 20,000 model soldiers; coach house
- Children's playground

Picnic area; &; gift shop; cafeteria

Open: Easter Sun to last Sun in Sep; Sun, Thu and Bank Hols 12.30–5 (house open 1–5.30)

Admission: Adult £2.50; Child £1; OAP £2

NORFOLK LAVENDER

Caley Mill, Heacham
Tel: 0485 70384
(2m S of Hunstanton, on A149)

- England's only lavender farm
- Lavender, herb, rose and river gardens
- Guided tours

Gifts; souvenirs; lavender products and plants; cottage tea room; &

Open: *Tearooms* Easter to end Sep, daily, 10–5.30 *Grounds and shop* all year, Mon–Fri, 9–4

Admission: free; *guided tours* Adults 70p; children free; *coach trips to fields during harvest* £1 per person

NORFOLK WILDLIFE PARK

Gt Witchingham
Tel: 060544 274
(12m NW of Norwich, off A1067)

- Largest collection of British and European wildlife in Britain
- Trained reindeer (stars of the film 'Santa Claus – The Movie') pulling sledges around the park most afternoons
- Children's play area; pets' corner
- Waterfowl lakes; walk-through aviaries; peacock lawn

Tea room; gift shop; picnic areas

Open: daily 10.30–6 (or sunset)

Admission: Adult £2; Child £1; OAP £1.80

OTTER TRUST

Earsham
Tel: 0986 3470
(just off A143, 1½m W of Bungay)

- Britain's biggest collection of otters
- Lakes with water-fowl; woods with Muntjac deer and Chinese water deer
- Riverside walks
- Mobile Information Centre, with otters and wetlands theme

Picnic areas; tea room; gift shop

Open: Apr–end Oct, daily, 10.30–6

Admission: Adult £2; Child £1; OAP £1.50

SANDRINGHAM HOUSE

Tel: 0553 772675
(8m NE of King's Lynn)

- Royal residence with fine grounds
- Museum of motor cars and dolls
- Various exhibits, including some royal possessions
- Nature trail and lake
- Adventure playground

Restaurant; café; &; *tea room; shop*

Open: Apr–Sep, Mon–Thur, 11–5 (Sun 12–5); house closed 2 weeks July/Aug

Admission: *House and grounds* Adult £2; Child £1.50; OAP £1.20 *Grounds only* Adult £1.50; Child £1.10; OAP 80p

THRIGBY HALL WILDLIFE GARDENS

Tel: 049377 477
(6m NW of Great Yarmouth off A1064)

* Large hall, lake and special collection of Asian mammals, birds and reptiles, in landscaped gardens
* Tropical house; snow leopards; bird house; deer paddocks
* Free slide show
* Children's play area

Cafeteria; gift shop (seasonal only)

Open: all year, daily, 10–5 or dusk

Admission: Adult £2; Child £1; OAP £1.50

THURSFORD COLLECTION

Thursford
Tel: 032877 477
(6m NE of Fakenham off A148)

* Large collection of steam road locomotives and engines
* 9 mechanical organs playing daily
* Weekly summer concerts on a Wurlitzer organ

Open: Easter–end Oct, daily, 2–5.30; special events during Dec

Admission: Adult £2.40; Child £1; OAP £2.15

WOLFERTON STATION

Tel: 0485 40674
(on Sandringham Estate, 5m NE of King's Lynn)

* Unique museum of Edwardian Royal travel housed in former Royal Retiring Rooms, at disused Sandringham station
* Relics from royal trains, such as Queen Victoria's tiny travelling bed
* Victorian and Edwardian clothes and documents
* Guided tours

Gift shop; &

Open: daily excluding Sat, Apr–end Sep; Mon–Fri, 11–1 and 2–5.30; Sun 2–5.30

Admission: Adult £1; Child 40p; OAP 90p; disabled 80p

The Imperial War Museum, Duxford (page 46)

SUFFOLK

EASTON FARM PARK

Tel: 0728 746475
(2½m N of Wickham Market; turn off A12 on to B116 and follow Easton signs)

- Victorian working farm, with animals and vintage farm machinery
- Suffolk Punch horses and blacksmith's shop
- Animals for children to feed
- Herd of 130 dairy cows, and afternoon milking
- Pets' corner and adventure play pit

Picnic area; tea shop; craft and country bygones shop

Open: Easter to end Oct, daily, 10.30–6

Admission: Adult £2; Child £1; OAP £1.50; reduced admission and facilities on Sat

PLEASUREWOOD HILLS AMERICAN THEME PARK

Tel: 0502 513626/7
(12m N of Lowestoft, off A12)

- American-style theme park, with wide variety of attractions
- Thrill rides; water fantasy rides; Ladybird coaster; Pirate ship
- Miniature railway; veteran car rides; fantasy canal rides
- Parrot show; sea-lion show
- Cine 180; boating lake
- Pets' corner; nature trail; children's playground

Picnic area; free wood-fired barbecues; crafts centre; &; baby-changing facilities; restaurant; café

Open: end April–3rd week May, weekends only; 19 May–11 Sep, daily, 10–6; weekends only till 25 Sep

Admission: Adult/Child £5; (under-threes free); OAP £2.90

EAST MIDLANDS

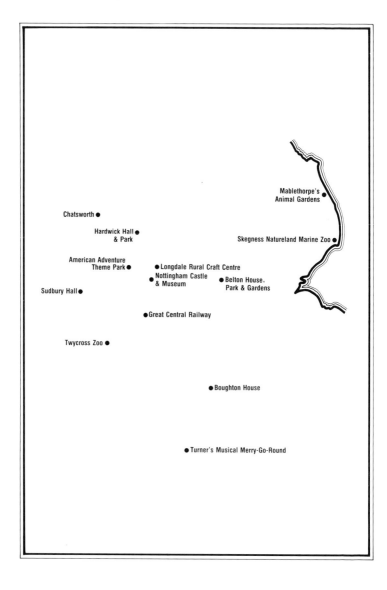

Mablethorpe's
Animal Gardens ●

Chatsworth ●

Hardwick Hall ●
& Park

Skegness Natureland Marine Zoo ●

American Adventure
Theme Park ●   ● Longdale Rural Craft Centre
● Nottingham Castle   ● Belton House,
& Museum   Park & Gardens

Sudbury Hall ●

● Great Central Railway

Twycross Zoo ●

● Boughton House

● Turner's Musical Merry-Go-Round

LEICESTERSHIRE

GREAT CENTRAL RAILWAY

Loughborough
Tel: 0509 230726
(in Great Central Road, just off A60 at southern end of town)

- Private steam railway operating over 5 miles
- Museum and locomotive depot at Loughborough
- Special events, including dining trains

Station buffet; 1st-class dining car on train; &; board at Quorn or Rothley; shop at Loughborough

Open: all year; Sat, Sun and Bank Hol Mon and Tue, 10–6 summer, 11–5 winter; also Wed and Thur in season (12–5) and Tue (12–5) Jul–Sep

Admission: (including return round trip from any station): Adult £2.50; Child/OAP £1; *Family Ticket* £5.50

TWYCROSS ZOO

Tel: 0827 880250/880440
(on A444, NW of Twycross; junction 18 on M1 from S; junction 23 on M1 from N)

- Large collection of wildlife in spacious open parkland
- One of the finest collections of monkeys and apes in England
- Enchanted Forest; bush dog, mongoose and capybara enclosure
- Summer events: Rio Grande railway; donkey rides; sea-lion feeding; chimps picnic, etc.
- Adventure playground; pets' corner

Large self-service cafeteria; licensed bar; tea bar open in winter; shop; picnic areas; & most days

Open: all year, 10–4.30

Admission: Adult £2.50; Child £1.20; OAP £2; Disabled £1

LINCOLNSHIRE

BELTON HOUSE, PARK AND GARDENS

Belton, Grantham
Tel: 0476 66116
(in village of Belton, just off main A607, 2½m NE of Grantham)

- 17th-century mansion built in the style of Sir Christopher Wren
- Fine collection of paintings; wood carvings; furniture; china; silver
- Unique momentoes of Duke of Windsor
- 1000 acres of beautiful parkland
- Formal gardens with orangery
- Extensive adventure playground
- Boat trips and miniature railway in summer

Riverside picnic area; National Trust shop and restaurant; & grounds only

Open: Apr–Oct, Wed–Sun and Bank Hol Mons, 1–5.30 (restaurant and gardens from 12); Last admission, 5

Admission: Adult £2.60; Child £1.30

MABLETHORPE'S ANIMAL GARDENS

North End, Mablethorpe
Tel: 0521 73346
(opposite Golden Sands Estates)

- Over 200 animals in gardens and natural dunes
- Emphasis on the breeding of small mammals, e.g. racoons
- Recuperating injured and sick animals and birds, e.g. seals; owls
- Walk-through aviary

Tea gardens; &

Open: early Mar–early Oct, daily, 10–6 (or 1 hour before dusk)

Admission: Adult £1.40; Child 70p; OAP £1

SKEGNESS NATURELAND MARINE ZOO

The Promenade, Skegness
Tel: 0754 4345

- Sea-lions; performing seals; baby seals; penguins
- Aquarium with tropical fish
- Tropical House with crocodiles; snakes; scorpions; giant African snails
- Floral Palace with free-flight tropical birds
- Children's pets' corner
- Walk-through tropical butterfly house
- Animal brass rubbing house

Refreshments; & *except Tropical House and toilets*

Open: all year daily (except Christmas Day); Apr–Sep, 10–6; Jul, Aug, 10–7.30; Oct–Apr, 10–5

Admission: Adult £1.60; Child/ OAP 80p

NORTHAMPTONSHIRE

BOUGHTON HOUSE

Kettering
Tel: 0536 515731
(3m N of Kettering)

- 500-year-old monastic building, converted into Versailles-like mansion in 1695
- Outstanding collection of 17th- and 18th-century French and English furniture; tapestries; armoury; ceilings; paintings; drawings
- State coach on view in coach house
- Beautiful parkland with avenues and lakes
- Woodland play area

Picnic area; teas; craft and garden shops; &

Open: Aug, daily, *Grounds* 12–6, *House* 2–5 (last admissions 4.30); *Grounds, nature trail, kitchen garden, plant stall* May–Sep, daily, except Fri, 12–5

Admission: Adult £2; Child/OAP £1.50; *Grounds only:* Adult 80p; Child/OAP 60p

TURNER'S MUSICAL MERRY-GO-ROUND

Queen Eleanor Vale, Wootton
Tel: 0604 763314
(S of Northampton on B526 Newport Pagnell road)

- Entertainment for all ages, with fairground carousel; concerts on the mighty Wurlitzer; ballroom dancing

- Unique collection of mechanical musical instruments
- Nostalgic tea dances, as well as discos
- Rides on the giant carousel

Licensed bar; cream teas; &

Open: all year; *Musical show/Sing-along/Dancing* Tues–Thur, 2–5; *Sight and sound spectacular* Sun and Bank Hols at Easter, Spring and Aug, 2–5; *supper dance parties* Fri and Sat, 8–12; *Wurlitzer concerts* on selected Weds 7.45–22.30

Admission: by pre-booking except Sun and Bank Hols; prices vary according to events

Longdale Rural Craft Centre (page 56)

NOTTINGHAMSHIRE

LONGDALE RURAL CRAFT CENTRE

Longdale Lane, Ravenshead
Tel: 0623 794858/796952
(off A60, 8m N of Nottingham, near Papplewick Pumping Station)

- Re-created village streets, with craftsmen at work
- Saddlery; weaving; woodcarving; pottery; silversmith; etc.

Gallery with crafts for sale; coffee lounge/restaurant; &

Open: all year, daily (except 25/26 Dec), 9–6

Admission: (to Working Craft Museum): Adult 60p, Child 30p, OAP 45p

NOTTINGHAM CASTLE AND MUSEUM

Tel: 0602 411881
(in city centre)

- 17th-century residence, converted to a museum in 1878
- Fine ceramics; silver; glass; alabaster carvings
- Local historical, archaeological and ethnographical displays
- First floor gallery, with works by Nottingham-born artists
- Temporary exhibitions throughout the year
- Sherwood Foresters' Regimental Museum
- Special events on green during festival
- Conducted tours of underground passages every day except Sunday

Refreshments; museum shop; & *except Regimental Museum*

Open: all year, daily (except Christmas Day); Apr–Sep, 10–5.45; Oct–Mar, 10–4.45

Admission: free (except Sun and Bank Hols; Adult 20p, Child 10p)

SOUTH DERBYSHIRE

AMERICAN ADVENTURE THEME PARK

Ilkeston
Tel: 0773 769931
(between Heanor and Ilkeston on A6007; 5m from M1 (junction 26)

- 40,000 square feet of undercover fun and games
- Boat rides; railway; big wheel rides; slides
- Wild West Theme with Chief Sitting Bull, Hill Billy Shoot; adventure fort; Wild West wonderland for under-fives, etc.
- Restaurants and bars; souvenir shops; picnic and rest area

& *wheelchair rental; £1 gift voucher for OAPS*

Open: 10–6; Easter week and Bank Hols; weekends to end May; daily to end Sep; subject to weather, first two weekends Oct

Admission: £5.95

CHATSWORTH

Bakewell
Tel: 024 688 2204
(on B6012, off A619 and A6, 4m E of
Bakewell)

- Splendid 17th- and 18th-century
  home of Duke and Duchess of
  Devonshire
- Superb collection of pictures,
  drawings, books and furniture
- 100 acres of beautiful parkland,
  with gardens, lakes, fountains
- Temple of Flora botanical
  exhibition in Sculpture Gallery
- Farmyard with sheep, cattle,
  horses, pigs and other livestock
- Adventure playground

Home-made refreshments; & *garden and
farmyard*

Open: Apr–end Oct daily; *House*
11.30–4.30, *Garden* 11.30–5.00;
prebooked guided tours mid-week at
11

Admission: *House and gardens* Adult
£3.50; Child £1.75; OAP £2.75
Family Ticket £9 *Gardens only* Adult
£1.70; Child 85p; OAP £1.70

HARDWICK HALL AND PARK

Doe Lea, near Chesterfield
Tel: 0246 850430
(2m S of Chesterfield–Mansfield
Road A617, near M1 junction 29)

- Outstanding Elizabethan mansion
  built 1591–97 for the Countess of
  Shrewsbury (Bess of Hardwick)
- Fine collections of furniture,
  tapestries, and needlework
  exhibition
- Furniture and portraits of the
  Cavendish family

- Formal gardens, orchards and
  herb garden
- Country park with sheep and
  cattle

& *gardens only; shop; information
centre; lunches and teas in the Great
Kitchen*

Open: Apr–Oct, Wed, Thur, Sat,
Sun and Bank Hol Mon, 1–5.30 or
dusk (last admission to Hall 5); closed
Good Fri; access may be limited at
peak times to avoid congestion;
garden open daily during season,
12–5.30

Admission: *House and gardens* Adult
£3; Child £1.50 *Garden only* Adult
£1.30; Child 60p

SUDBURY HALL

Tel: 028 378 305
(in Sudbury village, 6m E of
Uttoxeter, off A50)

- Richly decorated Charles II house
- Museum of Childhood with
  imaginative displays about the life
  of children in the past; plenty of
  visitor participation
- Special events for children and
  adults

Tea rooms; & *grounds, museum,
tearooms (and hall, by prior
arrangement)*

Open: Apr–Oct, Wed–Sun and
Bank Hol Mon, 1–5.30 (last
admission 5); closed Good Fri

Admission: Adult £2.20; Child
£1.10; combined ticket for Hall and
Museum available

HEART OF ENGLAND

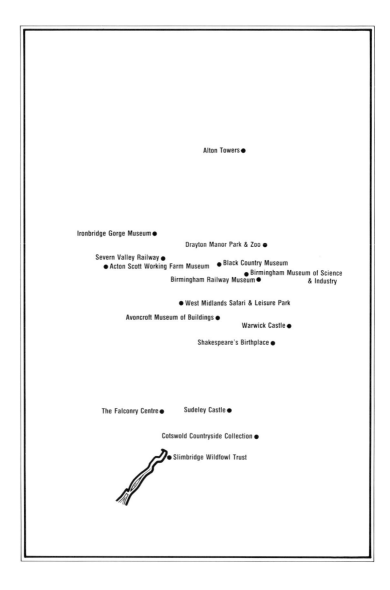

Alton Towers ●

Ironbridge Gorge Museum ●

Drayton Manor Park & Zoo ●

Severn Valley Railway ●
● Acton Scott Working Farm Museum   ● Black Country Museum
                                            ● Birmingham Museum of Science
Birmingham Railway Museum ●   & Industry

● West Midlands Safari & Leisure Park

Avoncroft Museum of Buildings ●
                                      Warwick Castle ●

Shakespeare's Birthplace ●

The Falconry Centre ●   Sudeley Castle ●

Cotswold Countryside Collection ●

● Slimbridge Wildfowl Trust

GLOUCESTERSHIRE

COTSWOLD COUNTRYSIDE COLLECTION

Northleach
**Tel: 0451 60715 (summer);
0285 655611 (winter)**
(W of Northleach, 10m NE of
Cirencester)

- Award-winning museum of
  agricultural history, housed in
  reconstructed cell block of what
  was once a House of Correction
- Wagons; horse-drawn implements;
  tools, etc.
- 'Below stairs' gallery

Open: Apr–Oct, daily, 10–5.30
(Sun, 2–5.30)

Admission: Adult 60p; Child 30p;
OAP 40p

THE FALCONRY CENTRE

Newent
Tel: 0531 820286
(1m SW of Newent off B4216)

- Largest collection of birds of prey
  in Europe
- Flying demonstrations daily,
  weather permitting, with eagles,
  falcons, etc.
- Breeding aviaries

Coffee shop; &

Open: Feb–Nov, daily, except
Tues, 10.30–5.30

Admission: Adult £2; Child £1.50

SUDELEY CASTLE

Winchcombe
Tel: 0242 602308
(off A46 between Cheltenham and
Broadway)

- 1,000 years of history; Katherine
  Parr lived and was buried here
- Fine collection of paintings
- Elizabethan garden
- Regular falconry displays
- Craft exhibition
- Guided tours
- Adventure playground for
  children
- Special events throughout the
  year; open-air theatre late June

Restaurant; & *gardens and ground floor
of castle*

Open: daily, Apr–Oct; *Grounds and
Craft Workshops* 11–5.30; *Castle* 12–5

Admission: Adults £3.25; Child
£1.75; OAP £2.75; *Family Ticket*
(2+2) £8

WILDFOWL TRUST

Slimbridge
Tel: 045389 333
(off A38, 12m S of Gloucester–M5
junction 13)

- World's biggest collection of
  wildfowl; over 2,300 birds of over
  180 different kinds, including wild
  swans, geese, ducks and flamingos
- Tropical house; exhibitions;
  cinema; comfortable hides

Catering facilities; gift shop; &

Open: all year, daily (except 24/25
Dec) 9.30–5 (or dusk)

Admission: Adult £2.80; Child
£1.30; OAP £2

HEREFORD & WORCESTER

AVONCROFT MUSEUM OF BUILDINGS

Stoke Heath
Tel: 0527 31886
(off the A38, SE of Bromsgrove)

- Interesting collection of reconstructed historic buildings, saved from destruction
- Working windmill; barn; granary; cockpit; 15th- and 16th-century timber-framed houses; Georgian ice house and earth closet
- Shire horse and wagon; newly erected toll house

Refreshments; shop; picnic area

Open: Mar–Nov; Jun–Aug, daily 11–5.30; Apr/May and Sep/Oct 11–5.30 (closed Mon); Mar and Nov 11–4.30 (closed Mon and Fri); open Bank Hols

Admission: Adult £1.90; Child 95p; OAP £1.10; *Family Ticket* £4.95

WEST MIDLANDS SAFARI AND LEISURE PARK

Tel: 0299 402114
(Spring Grove, on A456)

- 195 acres with wild animal reserves and Reptile House
- Amusement rides; roller coaster; pirate ship; boats; railway
- Sea-lion show
- Cine 180

Restaurant; picnic areas; &

Open: Apr–Oct, 10–5

Admission: Adult £6; Child (4–16) £5; under-fours free

SHROPSHIRE

ACTON SCOTT WORKING FARM MUSEUM

Wenlock Lodge, Acton Scott, near Church Stretton
Tel: 06946 306/7

- Working farm using heavy horses and 19th-century techniques
- Farm animals, including sheep, pigs, poultry
- Displays of traditional crafts like butter-making
- Farm produce for sale

Cafeteria; picnic site; &

Open: Apr–Oct, Mon–Sat 10–5 (Sun 10–6)

Admission: Adult £1.20 (peak season £1.50); Child/OAP 60p (75p)

IRONBRIDGE GORGE MUSEUM

Telford
Tel: 095 245 3522
(9m NW of Bridgnorth)

- History of industrial revolution in the Severn Gorge, spread over several sites
- Six museums including the Furnace and Iron Museum and Coalport China Museum, Blists Hill Open Air site
- Reconstructed Victorian village

Open: Apr–Oct, daily 10–6; Nov–Mar, daily (exc 24/25 Dec) 10–5

Admission: *All inclusive ticket:* Adult £4.95; Child £3.25

SEVERN VALLEY RAILWAY

Bridgnorth
Tel: 0299 403816 (24hr talking timetable 0299 401001)

- Fine collection of locomotives and rolling stock
- 16 miles of steam travel along valley of river Severn
- Unlimited travel for full journey ticket holders
- Sunday lunch and other meals on Restaurant Car Train

Catering facilities; real ale bars; souvenirs

Open: *station* all year, every day, 10–6; *trains* run daily May–Sep; Sats, Suns and Public Hols mid Mar–end Oct

Admission: Adult £1; Child 50p; Admission charges are refunded when a ticket for a train journey is purchased

STAFFORDSHIRE

ALTON TOWERS

Alton, near Ashbourne
Tel: 0538 702200
(12m E of Stoke, off B5032)

- Europe's premier leisure park, with over 100 attractions
- Former estate of the Earls of Shrewsbury, with splendid historic gardens
- Endless variety of rides, shows and live entertainment, including the Corkscrew, Grand Canyon Rapids Ride, Pirate ship, international circus, Skyride
- Collection of dolls, costumes and toys
- Kiddies Kingdom

Six restaurants; &; babychanging facilities

Open: daily 26 Mar–6 Nov, 10–5/6/7 (depending on season); *grounds* 9 till one hour after attractions close

Admission: (all-inclusive): Adult £7.99; Child £5.99 (children under 4 free)

DRAYTON MANOR PARK AND ZOO

Tamworth
Tel: 0827 287979
(on A5/A4091, S of Tamworth, close to M42)

- 160 acres of parkland, lakes and open-plan zoo
- Amusement park with 35 rides and attractions including Sky Wheel, Cine 180, Dinosaur Land, Looping Coaster, Pirate Ship, Cable Cars and lots more

&; cafeteria; shops; restaurant; bars; picnic areas; garden centre

Open: daily, Easter–Oct, 10.30–6

Admission: Adult £1.20, Child 60p (Wrist bands for unlimited rides or discount tickets available)

WARWICKSHIRE

SHAKESPEARE'S BIRTHPLACE

Henley Street, Stratford-upon-Avon
Tel: 0789 204016

- Half-timbered building, furnished in period style
- Collection of old books; manuscripts; memorabilia

- BBC TV Shakespeare costume exhibition

Open: daily (except Good Fri am, 24/25 Dec and 1 Jan); Apr–Oct, 9–6, Sun 10–6 (5 in Oct); Nov–Mar, 9–4.30, Sun 10–6

Admission: Adult £1.60; Child 60p (costume exhibition 20p/10p extra) *Inclusive ticket* to Anne Hathaway's Cottage, New Place (Shakespeare's last home), Hall's Croft (his daughter's home), Mary Arden's house (his mother's home): Adult £4.50; Child £2

WARWICK CASTLE

**Warwick
Tel: 0926 495421**

- One of the finest mediaeval castles in England
- State rooms; dungeon; torture chamber; Ghost Tower (and more)
- Madame Tussaud's unique exhibition: 'A Royal Weekend Party – 1898'
- 60 acres of grounds, with River Island, peacock gardens and walks

Licensed restaurant all year; light refreshments (Easter–Sep); Stables Restaurant Jul and Aug; &

Open: daily (except Christmas Day) 10–5.30 or 4.30 according to season

Admission: *all-inclusive ticket:* Adult £4, Child (5–16) £2.75, OAP £3.25; *Family Ticket* (2+2) £12 or (2+3) £13.50

WEST MIDLANDS

BIRMINGHAM MUSEUM OF SCIENCE AND INDUSTRY

**Newhall Street, Birmingham
Tel: 021-236 1022**

- Steam engines; cars and motorcycles; aircraft; demonstration machines
- Science and engineering
- Special steam days

&

Open: all year (except Christmas and New Year's day), Mon–Sat 9.30–5, Sun 2–5

Admission: free

BIRMINGHAM RAILWAY MUSEUM

**Steam Depot, Warwick Road, Tyseley
Tel: 021-707 4696**

- 12 steam locomotives; collection of specialist coaches; construction of workshop and other exhibits
- Special steam days first Sun each month and Bank Hols

Chuffs Railway Restaurant; Vintage Buffet Car and Royal Saloon Coach

Open: daily except 24/5 Dec and 1 Jan, 10–5 (or dusk);

Admission: Adult £1; Child/OAP 50p (Steam Days Adult £1.50–£2.50; Child/OAP 75p–£1)

West Midlands Safari and Leisure Park (page 60)

BLACK COUNTRY MUSEUM

Tipton Road, Dudley
Tel: 021-557 9643

- 26-acre open-air museum, with exhibits rebuilt from the Black Country
- Chainmaker's house and workshop
- Shops; chapel; canal; boat dock; coal mine and electric tramway
- Regular trips into Dudley Canal Tunnel

Restaurant; pub; cafeteria

Open: daily except Christmas Day, 10–5; reduced hours in winter

Admission: Adult £3; Child £2; OAP £2.50

63

WALES

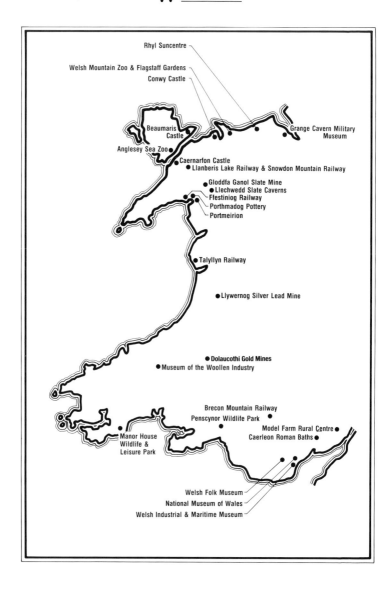

Rhyl Suncentre

Welsh Mountain Zoo & Flagstaff Gardens
Conwy Castle

Beaumaris
Castle

Grange Cavern Military
Museum

Anglesey Sea Zoo

Caernarfon Castle
Llanberis Lake Railway & Snowdon Mountain Railway

Gloddfa Ganol Slate Mine
Llechwedd Slate Caverns
Ffestiniog Railway
Porthmadog Pottery
Portmeirion

Talyllyn Railway

Llywernog Silver Lead Mine

Dolaucothi Gold Mines
Museum of the Woollen Industry

Brecon Mountain Railway
Penscynor Wildlife Park

Model Farm Rural Centre
Caerleon Roman Baths

Manor House
Wildlife &
Leisure Park

Welsh Folk Museum
National Museum of Wales
Welsh Industrial & Maritime Museum

CLWYD

GRANGE CAVERN MILITARY MUSEUM

Holway, Hollywell
Tel: 0352 713455
(on A55, 14m W of St Asaph)

- Large underground cavern, housing over 70 military vehicles, World War II bombs and huge collection of specialist items
- First World War battle trench; Falklands War display
- Video film theatre

Cafeteria; bar; souvenir shop; picnic areas

Open: Easter–end Oct, daily, 9.30–6 (last admission 5); closed Nov, Dec, Jan and Feb; re-opens during Mar, weekends only

Admission: Adult £1.95; Child £1.45; OAP £1.75

RHYL SUNCENTRE

East Parade, Rhyl
Tel: 0745 344433

- Holiday entertainment centre in a tropical island setting
- Surfing pool; roof-top monorail; leisure lagoon
- Children's splash pool; water chute; pool for toddlers
- Solarium sun-beds

Licensed lounge; self-service cafeteria; restaurant; shops; &

Open: Mar–Sep, daily, 10–11; Oct–Nov, Fri, Sat and Sun, 10–11

Admission: Adult £2.45; Child £1.50 (extra charges for some activities)

WELSH MOUNTAIN ZOO AND FLAGSTAFF GARDENS

Colwyn Bay
Tel: 0492 532938

- 37-acre site, with botanical gardens and panoramic views
- Daily displays of falconry; sea-lion feeding sessions
- Wide collection of animals, including lions; bears; elephants
- Jungle adventure land and bird shows
- Zoo minibus in summer

Restaurant; snack bar; bar; picnic sites; shop; &

Open: all year, 9.30–5 (except Christmas Day)

Admission: Adult £2.60; Child £1.30

DYFED

DOLAUCOTHI GOLD MINES

Pumsaint, Llanwrda
Tel: 05585 359
(just off A482 at Pumsaint)

- Gold mines on wooded hillsides overlooking beautiful valley
- Visitor Centre, with display, video and shop
- Walks around the Roman and modern gold mine
- Underground tours available in mid-summer
- Information Centre

Picnic site; shop

Open: Apr–Oct, 10–5

Admission: Adult £1.75; Child £1 *Tours* Adult £2.75; Child £1.75

LLYWERNOG SILVER LEAD MINE

Tel: 097 085 620
(on A44, near Ponterwyd)

- Large museum devoted to the history of gold, silver, lead and copper mining
- Audio-visual programme
- Steam pumping gear, with regular working days
- Floodlit cavern with Blue Pool

Refreshments; picnic site; craft centre; tourist information centre

Open: daily Easter–Oct 10–5 or 6 in high season

Admission: Adult £1.95; Child 95p; OAP £1.75

MANOR HOUSE WILDLIFE AND LEISURE PARK

Tel: 0646 651201
St Florence, 2m W of Tenby

- 12 acres of woods and gardens with monkeys, otters, birds, etc.
- Pets' corner and adventure playground
- Model railway exhibition; radio-controlled boats and cars
- Falconry displays

Souvenir shop; snack bar; licensed bar; &

Open: Easter–last weekend in Sep; daily 10–6

Admission: Adult £1.50; Child/OAP £1

MUSEUM OF THE WOOLLEN INDUSTRY

at Drefach–Felindrel
Tel: 0559 370929
(4m E of Newcastle Emlyn, off the A484)

- Major collection of traditional textile machinery and tools
- Exhibition of photographs tracing the wool industry
- Regular demonstrations of spinning, weaving, etc.

Restaurant; picnic site; shop

Open: Apr–Sep, Mon–Sat, 10–5; Oct–Mar, Mon–Fri, 10–5; closed Bank Holidays

Admission: free

GLAMORGAN

BRECON MOUNTAIN RAILWAY

Pant Station, Dowlais, Merthyr Tydfil
Tel: 0685 4854
(½m N of A465 at Merthyr Tydfil)

- 4-mile trip in narrow-gauge steam locomotive into Brecon Beacons National Park
- Locomotive museum and workshop

Lakeside tearoom; licensed restaurant; souvenir shop; picnic sites; &

Open: Most days Easter–end Sep, 11–5

Admission: Adult £2.60 return, child with adult free

NATIONAL MUSEUM OF WALES

Cathays Park, Cardiff
Tel: 0222 397951

- The story of Wales from early times
- Imaginative displays with Botany, Zoology, Geology, Industry, Art and Archaeology departments
- Outstanding collection of modern European paintings and sculpture

Restaurant; snack bar; shop

Open: Tue–Sat, 10–5, Sun 2.30–5; Closed Mon, Christmas, New Year's Day, Good Fri and May Day

Admission: free

PENSCYNOR WILDLIFE PARK

Cilfrew, Neath
Tel: 0639 2189
(off A465 at Aberdulais)

- Hundreds of animals and birds from all over the world
- Scenic chairlift to mountain top, and bobsleighs down

Cafeteria; snack bar; picnic site; shop; &

Open: all year, daily (weather permitting); closed Christmas Day; summer, 10–6; winter 10–4.30

Admission: Adult £2; Child/OAP £1

Caernarfon Castle (page 69)

WELSH FOLK MUSEUM

Cardiff
Tel: 0222 569441
(at St Fagans, 3m W of Cardiff;
junction 33 on M4)

- Large open-air museum of the life and culture of Wales
- Elizabethan mansion; formal gardens; Norman castle remains; farmhouses
- Tannery; forge; tollhouse; chapel; working woollen and flourmills
- Craft demonstrations on Saturdays throughout summer

Licensed restaurant; snack bar, picnic site; shop

Open: daily, 10–5; closed Christmas, New Year's Day, Good Fri, Suns in winter

Admission: Adult £2; Child £1; OAP £1.50

WELSH INDUSTRIAL AND MARITIME MUSEUM

Bute Street, Cardiff
Tel: 0222 481919

- The story of two centuries of industry in South Wales
- Many large outdoor exhibits, including pilot cutter, cranes, canal boat and working locomotives
- Steam days on first Saturdays of every month

Shop; &

Open: Tue–Sat, 10–5; Sun, 2–5.30; closed Mon, Christmas, New Year's Day, Good Fri and May Day

Admission: free

GWENT

CAERLEON ROMAN BATHS

Tel: 0633 422518
(1m N of Newport; M4 junction 25)

- Roman remains, including amphitheatre, the only fully excavated Roman barracks building in Britain, and Fortress Baths
- Interpretive displays provided by National Museum of Wales

Shop

Open: mid-March–mid-Oct, 9.30–6.30 (Sun 2–6.30); rest of year 9.30–4 (Sun 2–4); Closed 24/25 Dec and 1 Jan

Admission: Adult 75p; OAP/Child 35p

MODEL FARM RURAL CENTRE

Wolvesnewton, Chepstow
Tel: 02915 231
(1½ m from Llangwm off B435 Usk to Chepstow road)

- Victorian bygones among 27 acres of beautiful countryside
- Horse-drawn vehicles; agricultural equipment
- Workshops and working craftsmen
- Quiz trail for children
- Farm animals; adventure playground and lots more

Licensed restaurant; snack bar; picnic site; shop; &

Open: Easter–end Sep, daily, 11–6; Oct–Nov, weekends 11–6

Admission: Adult £1.85; Child £1; OAP £1.60; *Family Ticket* £5.25

GWYNEDD

ANGLESEY SEA ZOO

Brynsiencyn, Anglesey
Tel: 024 873 411
(on south shore of Anglesey, 6m
from Menai and Britannia Bridges)

- Unique collection of sea fish and
  plants, all under cover
- Big tanks of sharks, congers,
  skate, octopus, etc.
- Trout farming tank, where you
  can feed the fish

Snack bar; craft shop; seafood shop; &

Open: 13 Feb–early Nov, daily,
10–5; Jul and Aug, 9.30–5.30

Admission: Adult £1.95; Child 95p;
OAP £1.50

BEAUMARIS CASTLE

Tel: 0248 810361
(in centre of Beaumaris, on the Isle of
Anglesey)

- Last of the big castles, built by
  Edward I
- Excellent example of the British
  concentric castle
- Water-filled moat; refurbished
  chapel and special exhibition

Small shop

Open: summer, 9.30–6.30 (Sun,
2–6.30); winter, 9.30–4 (Sun 2–4)
closed Christmas and New Year's
Day

Admission: Adult £1; Child (5–16)
50p

CAERNARFON CASTLE

Tel: 0286 77617
(in centre of Caernarfon)

- Huge 13th-century castle built for
  Edward I
- 3 on-site exhibitions/museums
  and audio-visual presentation
- Walks around battlemented walls
  and visits to towers

& *parts of the castle only*

Open: daily, summer, 9.30–6.30
(Sun, 2–6.30); winter, 9.30–4 (Sun,
2–4); closed Christmas, New Year's
Day

Admission: Adult £2; Child/OAP
£1

CONWY CASTLE

Tel: 0492 592358
(in centre of Conwy, overlooking
Deganwy Estuary)

- Outstanding example of
  mediaeval European military
  architecture, built by Edward I
  1283–92
- Town Wall with 21 towers and 3
  main gateways

Souvenir shop

Open: mid-Mar–mid-Oct, daily,
9.30–6.30 (Sun, 2–6.30); rest of year,
9.30–4, (Sun, 2–4); closed Christmas,
New Year's Day

Admission: Adult £1; Child/OAP
50p

FFESTINIOG RAILWAY

Harbour Station, Porthmadog
Tel: 0766 512340/512384

- Narrow-gauge railway running through Snowdonia National Park
- Superb coastal and mountain scenery
- Most trains hauled by historic steam locomotives
- One-hour journey (each way)

Self-service restaurant and bar at Porthmadog; buffet service on train; shop; picnic area

Open: late Mar–end Oct, daily; also weekends in March and daily at Christmas and New Year

Admission: Adult 3rd class return £7, single £3.50; Child (5–15) with each paying adult free; under–5s free; any additional child £3.50 return, £1.75 single

GLODDFA GANOL SLATE MINE

Blaenau Ffestiniog
Tel: 0766 830664

- 'Largest slate mine in the world'
- Mining Museum with open-cast blasting
- Mills where slate is sawn and split for roofs, hearths, etc.
- Miners' cottages; Natural History Centre
- Narrow-gauge railway collection

Restaurant; snack bar; picnic site; bar; craft shop; &

Open: Easter–30 Sep, Mon–Fri 10–5.30; also Sunday mid-Jul–31 Aug; otherwise by arrangement

Admission: Adult £2.40; Child £1.20

LLANBERIS LAKE RAILWAY

Padarn Country Park, Llanberis
Tel: 0286 870549

- Steam train service along shores of Lake Padarn
- Magnificent views of Snowdonia
- Museum; Visitor Centre; walks; etc.

Cafeteria; picnic site; gift shop; &

Open: Easter–early Oct, Mon–Thur in low season (first 2 months), Sun–Fri in high season; trains run from 11–4.30

Admission: Adult £2.40 return; Child £1.20 return; reductions for families

LLECHWEDD SLATE CAVERNS

Blaenau Ffestiniog
Tel: 0766 830306
(on A470 North to South Wales trunk road)

- Two exciting rides underground into the slate mines
- Miners' Tramway tour of recreated Victorian conditions
- Deep Mine Tour, with tales of slate miners' lives
- Free exhibitions on the surface, such as slate splitting, smithy and tramway exhibitions

Cafeteria; pub and licensed restaurant; souvenir and gift shop; & Miners Tramway

Open: Apr–Oct, 10–5.15 (Oct 4.15); Nov–Mar by special arrangement

Admission: Adult £2.55; Child £1.60

PORTHMADOG POTTERY

Snowdon Street, Porthmadog
Tel: 0766 2137/2785

- Tours of working pottery
- Throw and paint a pot, and take it away
- Wales' largest wall mural (over 1,300 sq. ft.)

Picnic site; crafts shop (with some seconds and rejects); café

Open: week before Easter–Oct, Mon–Fri, 9–5.30

Admission: Adult 25p; Child free; throw/paint a pot £1.10

PORTMEIRION

Tel: 0766 770457
(off A470 between Porthmadog and Penrhyndeudraeth)

- Fantasy Italian-style village overlooking Cardigan Bay
- Beautiful site with woodlands, sub-tropical gardens and beaches
- Exhibition and audio-visual film show

Several shops (including Portmeirion Pottery seconds); restaurant; snack bar; picnic site; some parts accessible for &

Open: Easter–end Oct, daily, 9.30–5.30

Admission: Adult £1.80; Child 75p

SNOWDON MOUNTAIN RAILWAY

Llanberis
Tel: 0286 870223
(on A4086, 7½m from Caernarfon towards Capel Curig)

- Britain's only public rack-and-pinion railway
- Opened in 1896; climbs more than 3000 feet to top of Snowdon
- 2½-hour return trips to the top and back

Open: Mar 14–late Oct, (no weekend services late-season and certain weekends in Mar/Apr and May); in high season trains leave every 3 mins from 9 until 5 (3.15 Sat); at other periods service is reduced depending on weather and demand; trains go to the top from about mid-May to 1st week in Sep only; otherwise to Clogwyn and Rocky Valley

Fares: *normal return trip to summit* Adult £9.50; Child £6.50; special discounts on early morning trains; *single fares to peak* Adult £7; Child (under 15) £4.50

TALYLLYN RAILWAY

Wharf Station, Tywyn
Tel: 0654 710472
(on Cambrian coast, between Aberdovey and Barmouth)

- Rides on narrow-gauge steam trains (55 mins each way)
- Beautiful Welsh hill scenery
- Narrow-gauge railway museum
- Waterfalls and forest walks
- Educational facilities
- Christmas and New Year rides

Shops and refreshments at Wharf Station

Open: 28 Mar–Oct 30, most days, with limited services during early and late part of season

Return fare: Adult £3.60; Child £1.80; *Family Ticket (2+2)* £9

Yorkshire and Humberside

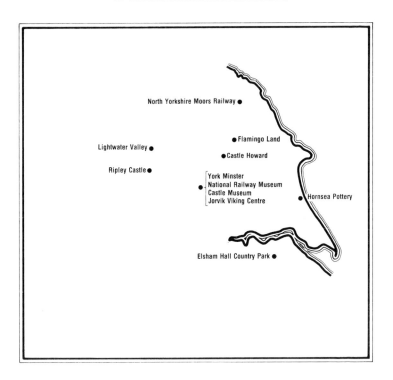

North Yorkshire Moors Railway ●

● Flamingo Land

Lightwater Valley ●

● Castle Howard

Ripley Castle ●

York Minster
National Railway Museum
Castle Museum
Jorvik Viking Centre

Hornsea Pottery ●

Elsham Hall Country Park ●

HUMBERSIDE

ELSHAM HALL COUNTRY PARK

Tel: 0652 688698
(near Brigg, 8m S of Humber Bridge)

- Animal garden; butterfly and bird gardens
- Carp lake
- Arts/crafts centre
- Adventure playground; nature trails; pony trekking
- Conservation/brass rubbing centre

Shop; light lunches; teas

Open: Easter Saturday to last weekend in Sep, daily, from 11, last admission 5.30; rest of year: Sun & Bank Holidays only, 11–4; closed Good Friday

Admission: Adult £1.90; Child 90p

HORNSEA POTTERY

Edenfield, Hornsea
Tel: 0964 532161
(13m NE of Hull)

- Leisure park in 30 acres of parkland on the coast
- Birds of prey; Butterfly World; adventure playground
- Remote control lorries and cars; water-borne dodgems
- Factory outlet shop with pottery seconds, glass, household linens, kitchen appliances, giftware and fashions
- Picturesque model village

Mother-and-baby room; &; *catering facilities; shops*

Open: Apr–Oct, daily from 10; Nov–Mar, shops only, Wed–Sun from 10

Admission: All inclusive price £2.99 (under–6 free); OAP £1.99

NORTH YORKSHIRE

CASTLE MUSEUM

Clifford Street, York
Tel: 0904 653611

- Outstanding museum of everyday objects, 1750–1980
- Everything from costume and arms to the kitchen sink
- Reconstructions of Victorian streets with stocked-up shops
- 1950s sitting room; juke box; radios; TVs

Tearoom

Open: Apr–Sep, Mon–Sat 9.30–5.30, Sun 10–5.30; Oct–Mar, Mon–Sat 9.30–4, Sun 10–4 (closed 25/26 Dec and 1 Jan)

Admission: Adult £2.25; Child/OAP £1.15

JORVIK VIKING CENTRE

Coppergate, York
Tel: 0904 643211

- Fascinating Viking city, with excavated houses and workshops
- Underground 'time-car' taking you back 1,000 years
- Recreated bustling market, dark, smoky houses and busy wharf
- Fascinating sites of the archaeological dig

&; *shop selling souvenirs, books and gifts with a historical slant*

Open: Apr–Oct, daily, 9–7; Nov–Mar, 9–5.30, daily (except Christmas Day) (last admission half an hour before closing)

Admission: Adults £2.75; Child (under 16) £1.35

NATIONAL RAILWAY MUSEUM

Leeman Road, York
Tel: 0904 21261

- 150 years of British Railway history
- Famous historic trains, locomotives and carriages
- 'Mallard', the holder of the World Speed Record for steam trains
- Picture gallery; audio-visual theatre; model railway

&; *Mother-and-baby room; gift shop; 'Buffers' Restaurant*

Open: Mon–Sat, 10–6, Sun 11–6 (closed 24/25/26 Dec and Jan 1)
Admission: Adults £1.50 ; Child (5–16) 75p; *Family Ticket* (2+3) £4

YORK MINSTER

York
Tel: 0904 622943

- Largest Gothic cathedral in England
- Superb mediaeval stained glass
- Restoration work still going on after fire 3½ years ago
- 275 steps up Central Tower for views of York
- Museum and Treasury presenting history of Minster

Open: 7–dusk, daily; *Undercroft Museum and Chapter House* 10–dusk (Sun 1–dusk); *Tower* as above, except Nov–Feb, weekends only

Admission: free; individual charges, *Chapter House* Adults 40p; Child 20p; *Central Tower* Adult £1.00; Child 50p; *Undercroft Museum* Adult 80p; Child 40p

CASTLE HOWARD

Coneysthorpe
Tel: 065 384 333
(off A64, 15m NE of York)

- Stunning 18th-century stately home
- Principal location for TV's Brideshead Revisited
- Outstanding paintings; furniture; china; tapestries
- Britain's largest privately owned collection of period costumes
- Delightful grounds with lakes, fountain and rose gardens
- Children's adventure playground

Cafeteria; plant centre; ⅃

Open: Mar 24–end Oct daily; *Grounds* and *plant centre* from 10; *House, costume galleries* and *cafeteria* 11–5 (last admission 4.30)

Admission: all-inclusive ticket, Adult £3.50; Child £1.50; OAP £2.80

FLAMINGO LAND

Kirby Misperton, Malton
Tel: 065 386 287

- Family funpark with over 100 attractions
- Zoo with lions, wolves, dolphins, polar bears, birds, etc.
- Children's farm; adventure playground
- Lots of rides, activities and shows

7 different places to eat; gift and sweet shops; mother's changing room; ⅃

Open: 27 Mar–2 Oct, 10–6

Admission: Adult/Child £4 (all-inclusive price); under-fives free

LIGHTWATER VALLEY

North Stainley
Tel: 0765 85321
(3m N of Ripon)

- Visitor farm with animals and modern farming methods
- 125-acre park with steam-drawn train, fairground, BMX track, and lots more activities
- Boating lake; adventure playground

Restaurant; cafeteria; picnic areas

Open: 1st Apr for a week; weekends only until May; weekends, Weds, Thurs in May; end May–6 Sep, daily

Admission: Adult/Child £4.95; under-threes free

NORTH YORKSHIRE MOORS RAILWAY

Pickering Station
Tel: 0751 73791

- Steam travel through North York Moors National Park
- 18 miles, with several stops en route
- Dinners served on North Yorkshire Pullman on summer evenings

Station shops and refreshments at Pickering, Goathland and Grosmont; refreshments on most trains

Open: 26 Mar–30 Oct also Santa Specials in Dec (weekends); ring for times

Admission: from 26 June–3 Sep: Adult return £5; Child £2.30. Before 26 June and after 3 Sep: Adult £4.50; Child £2.30; OAP £3.05

RIPLEY CASTLE

Ripley
Tel: 0423 770152
(4m N of Harrogate on A61 Ripon road)

- 16th–18th-century ancestral home of Ingilby family
- Guests have included James I and Oliver Cromwell
- Contents ranging from fine porcelain to priests' hiding hole
- Walled garden and grounds with lake and park views
- Playground

Various shops and stores; Castle Tea Room; licensed restaurant

Open: 1 Apr–16 Oct; weekends only Apr, then closed every Mon until Oct 16th

Admission: Adult £2; Child 80p; OAP £1.85

Jorvik Viking Centre, York (page 73)

NORTHUMBRIA

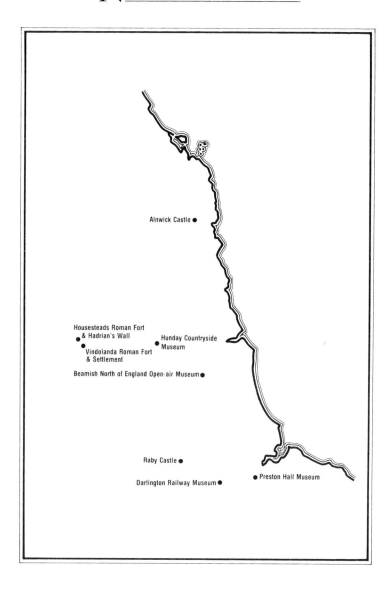

Alnwick Castle ●

Housesteads Roman Fort
● & Hadrian's Wall
●
Vindolanda Roman Fort
& Settlement

Hunday Countryside
● Museum

Beamish North of England Open-air Museum ●

Raby Castle ●

Darlington Railway Museum ●

● Preston Hall Museum

CLEVELAND

PRESTON HALL MUSEUM

Stockton
Tel: 0642 781184
(off the A135 between Stockton-on-Tees and Yarm)

- Social history museum, with armour, costumes, toys, etc.
- 'Period street' with working craftsmen

Open: Mon to Sat, 9.30–5.30 (Sun 2–5.30); last admission 5; closed Christmas and Good Fri

Admission: free

DURHAM

BEAMISH NORTH OF ENGLAND OPEN-AIR MUSEUM

Tel: 0207 231811
(8m S of Newcastle-upon-Tyne, near A1(M). Take Chester-le-Street turn-off from A1(M) and follow museum signs along A693 towards Stanley)

- European Museum of the Year, 1987
- Open-air museum of northern life in the 1920s
- Reconstructed 1920s High Street, with shops, inn, etc.
- Home farm, with exhibitions, pigs, cattle, hens
- Life at the pithead, with pit cottages and pit ponies
- Railway station with steam locomotive

Tea room (summer only); gift shop; picnic area

Open: Apr–Oct, daily, 10–6; Nov–Mar, daily (except Mon), 10–5; last admission always 4 &

Admission: Adult £3.30; Child/OAP £2.30; Disabled free

DARLINGTON RAILWAY MUSEUM

North Road Station, Darlington
Tel: 0325 460532
(¾m N of town centre, just off A167)

- Restored station, dating from 1842
- Historic steam locomotives including Stephenson's 'Locomotion'
- Exhibits relating to railways of NE England

Light refreshments; souvenir shop; &

Open: daily (except Christmas and New Year) 9.30–5

Admission: Adult 80p; Child 40p; OAP 50p

RABY CASTLE

Tel: 0833 60202
(off A688, just N of Staindrop)

- Mediaeval castle with Victorian additions in 200-acre park
- Paintings; furniture; 600-year-old kitchen; carriage collection
- Walled gardens and deer in park

Tea rooms in stables

Open: Easter Sat–following Wed; May–June, Wed and Sun only; July–Sep, Sun–Fri and Bank Hol Sat; *castle 1–5, park and gardens 11–5.30*

Admission: *castle* Adult £2; Child/OAP £1.20, *grounds only* Adult 80p; Child 50p

NORTHUMBERLAND

ALNWICK CASTLE

Tel: 0665 602207

- Splendid border fortress belonging to Duke and Duchess of Northumberland
- Collection of paintings; porcelain; armour
- Dungeon; state coach and museum
- Garden by Capability Brown

Open: 30 Apr–30 Sep, daily Sun–Fri and Bank Hol Sats, 1–5; last admission 4.30

Admission: Adult £2; Child 90p; OAP £1.50

HOUSESTEADS ROMAN FORT AND HADRIAN'S WALL

Tel: 04984 363
(6m NE of Haltwhistle on B6318)

- 5-acre garrison fort (best preserved of Roman forts)
- Numerous remains, including latrine with flushing tank
- Walks along the Wall, and fine views
- Small site museum and information centre

Open: summer, 10–6, Mon–Sat (2–6 Sun) winter, 10–4, Mon and Sat

Admission: Adult £1.25; Child 60p; OAP 95p

HUNDAY COUNTRYSIDE MUSEUM

Newton
Tel: 0661 842553
(3m east of Corbridge, 14m W of Newcastle on A69)

- Over 200 vintage tractors and engines
- Old farmhouse kitchen and other domestic memorabilia
- Working, water-powered cornmill
- Narrow-gauge railway
- Farm animals

Tea room; gift shop

Open: daily Apr–Oct, 10–6; last admission 5

VINDOLANDA ROMAN FORT AND SETTLEMENT

Bardon Mill
Tel: 04984 277
(26m E of Carlisle, 14m W of Hexham)

- Lively museum in ornamental gardens
- Full-scale reconstruction of sections of Hadrian's Wall
- Roman remains

Café

Open: daily, from 10–4 (mid-Oct–mid-Mar), 10–5 or 6.30 at other times of year

Admission: Adult £1.50; Child 80p; OAP £1.25

Beamish North of England Open-air Museum (page 77)

THE NORTH WEST

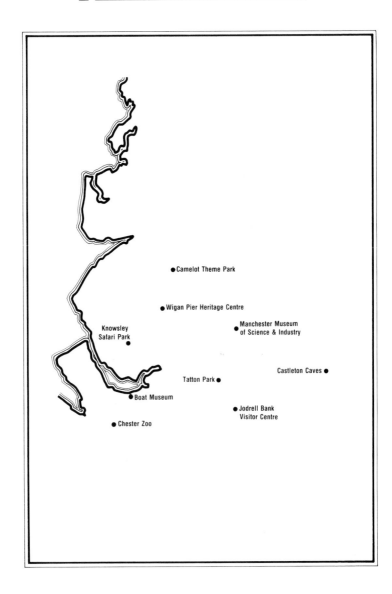

Camelot Theme Park

Wigan Pier Heritage Centre

Knowsley
Safari Park

Manchester Museum
of Science & Industry

Castleton Caves

Tatton Park

Boat Museum

Jodrell Bank
Visitor Centre

Chester Zoo

CHESHIRE

THE BOAT MUSEUM

Ellesmere Port
Tel: 051355 5017
(7m N of Chester at Ellesmere Port, off M53)

- Award-winning dockland museum with over 50 canal craft
- Craft workshops and exhibitions on canal development
- Regular boat trips and two steam engines in steam on first Sunday of each month and Bank Holidays

Cafeteria; souvenir shop; picnic area; &

Open: 11–5 (winter 10–4 and closed on Friday and Christmas Day)

Admission: Adult £2.50; Child £1.40; OAP £1.80; *Family Ticket* £7

CHESTER ZOO

Tel: 0244 380280
(signposted from M56 and all major roads in the area)

- One of the country's best zoos with over 3,000 animals, including rare and endangered species
- 110 acres of garden with thousands of different bedding plants
- Tropical house
- Waterbus rides

Catering facilities; &

Open: daily, from 10

Admission: Adult £3.50; Child/OAP £1.75

JODRELL BANK VISITOR CENTRE

Tel: 0477 71339
(near Holmes Chapel on A535; junction 18 off M6)

- Exhibition on space and astronomy
- One of the world's largest radio telescopes
- Working models; video shows; light and laser displays
- Two planetarium shows which carry you through the universe
- 35-acre Tree Park

Picnic area; licensed restaurant; shop

Open: Easter–end Oct, daily, 10.30–5.30; winter weekends, 2–5

Admission: Adult £2.50; Child £1.25; OAP £2

MANCHESTER MUSEUM OF SCIENCE AND INDUSTRY

Liverpool Road, Castlefield, Manchester
Tel: 061 832 2244

- Industry in action
- Power Hall with motive power through the ages
- Air and Space Gallery; Electricity Gallery, etc.

Licensed buffet; gift shop; & *access to much of the site*

Open: daily, 10–5

Admission: Adult £1; Child 50p

TATTON PARK

Tel: 0565 54822/3
(3½m from M6 junction 19)

- Beautiful Georgian mansion
- Newly opened cellars providing Victorian working atmosphere
- 60 acres of superb gardens and huge deer park
- Museum with state coach, veteran vehicles and hunting trophies
- 1930s Working Home Farm

Gift shop; restaurant

Open: *park and gardens* daily (except Christmas Day and 21/22 June); *mansion and farm,* Apr–end Oct, Suns only Nov and Mar

Admission: Adult £1.25; *garden* 90p; *mansion* 95p; *farm* 90p; Child roughly half price

LANCASHIRE

CAMELOT THEME PARK

Park Hall, Charnock Richard, Chorley, Preston
Tel: 0257 452090

- Over 80 rides and entertainments
- Castle; cave; Indian village; Arthurian knights; wizards and dragons
- Live jousting tournaments
- Spanish holiday village
- Live shows; family rides; adventure playground; etc.

Nappy changing room; picnic areas; restaurant; bars; &

Open: 26 Mar–10 Apr, 10–6; 16 Apr–29 May, weekends and Bank Holidays only; 30 May–25 Sep, daily; 1 Oct–6 Nov, weekends only

Admission: £4.95; under–threes free; *Family Ticket* (2 + 2) £15.95

WIGAN PIER HERITAGE CENTRE

Tel: 0942 323666 (24–hour information 0942 44888)

- 'The way we were' – exhibition of life in Wigan in the year 1900, with company of actors
- Trencherfield Mill, with exhibition of working history, textile machinery and largest steam engine in the world

Café; pub; restaurant; shop; gardens

Open: all year (except Christmas Day and Boxing Day), 10–5

Admission: Adult £2; Child/OAP £1

MERSEYSIDE

KNOWSLEY SAFARI PARK

Tel: 051 430 9009
(A58 between Prescot and Knowsley)

- Drive-through game reserves with lions, tigers, elephants, white rhinos and other exotic animals
- Dolphinarium
- Children's amusement park and pet's corner

Cafeteria with small bar; picnic areas; souvenir shop

Open: mid-Feb to 31 Oct, 10–4

Admission: Car £6; *Safari Bus* Adult £2.50; Child £1.50; OAP £2

NORTH DERBYSHIRE

CASTLETON CAVES
Peak Cavern

Tel: 0433 20285

- Large cave with stalactites and underground river

Open: 10–5 daily

Admission: Adult £1.55; Child 80p

Speedwell Cavern

Tel: 0433 20512

- Old lead mine with mile-long boat ride

Open: 9.30–5.30, daily

Admission: Adult £3; Child £2

Treak Cliff Cavern

Tel: 0433 20571

- Extensive cave system with rare stalactites and stones

Open: daily, 9.30–6 summer; 9.30–4 winter

Admission: Adult £1.90; Child 90p; OAP £1.20

Blue John Cavern and Mine

Tel: 0433 20642

- Large range of natural caves with richly coloured stalactites

Open: daily in season, from 9.45

Admission: Adult £2; Child £1

Wigan Pier Heritage Centre

CUMBRIA

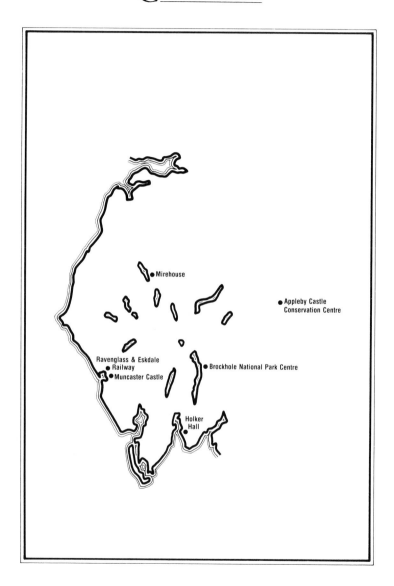

APPLEBY CASTLE CONSERVATION CENTRE

Appleby
Tel: 07683 51402
(12m S of Penrith on A66)

- Beautiful riverside setting for rare breeds of British farm animals, waterfowls, owls, parrakeets, raccoons and deer
- Fine 11th-century Norman Keep
- Nature trail; Tarzan trail

Tea rooms; gift shop

Open: Good Fri–end Sep, daily, 10–5

Admission: Adult £2; Child/OAP £1

BROCKHOLE NATIONAL PARK CENTRE

Brockhole, Windermere
Tel: 096 62 6601
(between Windermere and Ambleside on A591)

- Large lakeside gardens and nature trails
- Audio-visual presentations on the Lake District
- Lots of printed information on the Lake District
- Special children's events during school holidays
- Boat trips in summer; nature trail; play area
- Beatrix Potter Grotto and Living Lakeland exhibitions

Picnic areas; shop; café

Open: daily, late Mar–early Nov; from 10

Admission: Adult £1.30; Children 60p

HOLKER HALL

Cark-in-Cartmel
Tel: 044 853 328
(5m W of Grange-over-Sands)

- Fine country estate, former home of the Dukes of Devonshire
- Large gardens; deer park; sheep; animal house
- Craft museum; motor museum; model train display
- Victorian/Edwardian Kitchen Exhibition
- Adventure playground
- Various annual events including horse trials and hot-air balloon championships

Cafe; gift shop; &

Open: Easter Sun to last Sun in Oct, daily except Sat, 10.30–6; last admission to Hall and grounds 4.30

Admission: Adult from £1.80; Child from £1

MIREHOUSE

Tel: 07687 72287
(4½m N of Keswick on A591 towards Carlisle)

- Beautiful 17th-century Manor House connected with Bacon, Wordsworth and Tennyson
- Original furniture
- Adventure playgrounds
- Woodland and lakeside walks

Home-made food in converted sawmill

Open: Apr–Oct; *house* Suns, Weds, Bank Hol Mons, 2–5; *grounds and tearoom* daily, 10.30–5.30

Admission: Adult £1.60; Child 80p *grounds only* Adult 60p; Child 40p

MUNCASTER CASTLE

Ravenglass
Tel: 06577 614
(on A595, 1m SE of Ravenglass)

- Mediaeval castle in beautiful gardens
- Guided tours by the family who live there
- Himalayan bear garden; wallabies; bird garden

Gift shop; refreshments; garden centre

Open: Apr–Sep, Tue–Sun, *grounds* 12–5, *house* 1.30–4.30

Admission: *house & garden* Adult £2.50; Child £1.25; *grounds only* Adult £1.25; Child 70p

RAVENGLASS AND ESKDALE RAILWAY

Ravenglass
Tel: 06577 226
(on A595 coast road)

- Miniature railway covering 7 miles of glorious countryside
- Railway Museum

Open: Regular services all season and a reduced service during winter. Ring for timetable details

Fares: Adult £3.80; Child £1.90; *Family Ticket* £9.50

Holker Hall (page 85)

86

SCOTLAND

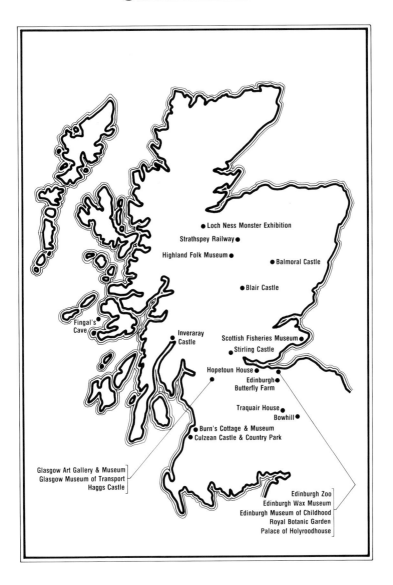

Loch Ness Monster Exhibition

Strathspey Railway

Highland Folk Museum

Balmoral Castle

Blair Castle

Fingal's Cave

Inveraray Castle

Scottish Fisheries Museum

Stirling Castle

Hopetoun House

Edinburgh Butterfly Farm

Traquair House

Bowhill

Burn's Cottage & Museum

Culzean Castle & Country Park

Glasgow Art Gallery & Museum
Glasgow Museum of Transport
Haggs Castle

Edinburgh Zoo
Edinburgh Wax Museum
Edinburgh Museum of Childhood
Royal Botanic Garden
Palace of Holyroodhouse

BORDERS

BOWHILL

Selkirk
Tel: 0750 20732
(off A708, 3m W of Selkirk)

- Outstanding collection of paintings, porcelain and furniture
- Adventure woodland play area; riding centre
- Garden; nature trails

Tea room; gift shop

Open: *House* early Jul to mid-Aug, daily 1–4.30; *grounds and playgrounds* May–Aug, daily except on the Fridays when the house is closed, 12–5 (Sun, 2–6)

Admission: *house and grounds* Adult £2.50; Child £1.00; *grounds only* Adult £1.00; Child £1.00

TRAQUAIR HOUSE

Innerleithen
Tel: 0896 830323
(B709, off A72, 8m ESE of Peebles)

- Oldest continuously inhabited house in Scotland (dating back to 10th-century)
- Paintings; porcelain; manuscripts
- 18th-century brewhouse, where ale is regularly produced
- Woodland and River Tweed walks; maze; craft workshops

Restaurant/tearoom; gift shop; gallery; & partial access

Open: Easter; May 1–Sep 30, 1.30–5.30 (last admission 5.15)

Admission: Adult £2 (£2.50 Jul and Aug); Child £1

CENTRAL

STIRLING CASTLE

Tel: 0786 62517
(in central Stirling)

- Historic castle standing on a great rock
- Favourite Scottish royal residence from 14th century
- Much rebuilding, but parts go back to 16th century
- Renaissance Palace of James V, 16th-century Chapel Royal and Hall
- Visitor centre, with audio-visual display and shop

Tea garden and tea room (summer only); &

Open: all year, daily; summer 9.30–5 (Sun 10.30–4.15) winter 9.30–4.20 (Sun 12.30–3.35)

Admission: Adult £1.50; Child 75p; *Family Ticket* £4

FIFE

SCOTTISH FISHERIES MUSEUM

Anstruther Harbour
Tel: 0333 310628
(10m SSE of St Andrews)

- 16th- to 19th-century buildings; housing marine aquarium; fishing and ships gear; model and real fishing boats
- Fisher-home interior; reference library

Tea room

Open: all year, daily

Admission: Adult £1; Child/OAP 50p

GRAMPIAN

BALMORAL CASTLE

Tel: 03384 334
(on A93, 8m W of Ballater)

- Royal Family holiday home since the time of Queen Victoria
- Main part of castle closed to public but you can visit Ballroom Exhibition (in the castle)
- Gardens and grounds with country walks and pony-trekking

Souvenir shops; refreshment room; &

Open: May–Jul, daily except Sun, 10–5 (may be closed when members of the Royal Family are in residence)

Admission: Adult £1.20; Child free; OAP £1

HIGHLANDS

HIGHLAND FOLK MUSEUM

Kingussie
Tel: 05402 307
(on A9, 12m SW of Aviemore)

- Open-air exhibits including 18th-century shooting lodge, a mill, a turf-walled house and farming equipment
- Farming museum with a barn, dairy, stable, Highland tinkers
- Weapons; costume; musical instruments; Highland furniture
- Special events Easter–September
- Guided tours in winter

Picnic garden

Open: all year; Apr–Oct, Mon–Sat 10–6, Sun 2–6, last admission 5.30; Nov–Mar, Mon–Fri, 10–3

Admission: Adult £1.25; Child/OAP 65p

LOCH NESS MONSTER EXHIBITION

Drummadrochit
Tel: 04562 573
(on A82, 14m SW of Inverness)

- Fascinating story of the loch and its monster

&

Open: all year, daily (except Christmas day and New Year's day); from 9–5/9 depending on the month; winter, 10–4

Admission: Adult £1.65; Child (5–10) 75p; Child (11–16) £1; OAP £1.20

STRATHSPEY RAILWAY

Tel: 047983 692
(access at Aviemore (Speyside) or Boat of Garten)

- Passenger steam service from Aviemore to Boat of Garten
- Splendid scenery with mountains and forest
- Museum of static rolling stock and relics at Boat of Garten

Open: Easter weekend and weekends May–Oct; also Mon, Tue, Wed from mid-Jun to Aug; ring for times of trains

Fares: three classes, single and returns, at various prices from £1.20. Children half price. Family Return available on third class only, £6

LOTHIAN

EDINBURGH BUTTERFLY FARM

Tel: 031 663 4932
(6m E of Edinburgh on A7 towards
Dalkeith)

- Large greenhouse, with lush
  tropical plants, cascading
  waterfalls and lily ponds
- Butterflies from all over the world
- Exotic insects; photographic
  displays
- Children's playground

*Tea room; garden centre; tropical fish
shop; picnic area*

Open: 25 March–31 Oct, daily,
10–5.30

Admission: Adult £1.75; OAP
£1.00; Child (5–16) £1.00; Under-
fives free; *Family Ticket* £5.00

EDINBURGH MUSEUM OF CHILDHOOD

High Street, Royal Mile
Tel: 031 225 1131

- Unique collection of toys, dolls,
  dolls' houses, costumes, etc.

Open: 10–5, all year; closed Sun and
public holidays

Admission: free

Edinburgh Butterfly Farm

EDINBURGH WAX MUSEUM

142 High Street, Royal Mile
Tel: 031 226 4444

- Models of prominent Scottish figures
- Mary Queen of Scots, Robert Burns, Ronnie Corbett, Lulu, etc.
- Chamber of Horrors
- 'Never-Never Land' with fairytale characters

Open: daily (except Christmas Day), Apr–Sep 10–7; Oct–Mar 10–5

Admission: Adult £2.25, Child 80p

EDINBURGH ZOO

Tel: 031 334 9171
(entrance from Corstorphine Road (A8), 4m W of city centre)

- Large and varied collection of mammals, birds and reptiles
- Famous for large breeding colony of Antarctic Penguins
- Adventure playground

Restaurants; bars; shops; &

Open: 9–dusk daily

Admission: Adult £2.60; Child £1.30

HOPETOUN HOUSE

Tel: 031 331 2451
(W of South Queensferry)

- Great Adam mansion, now home of Marquesses of Linlithgow
- Notable paintings, including Rubens, Rembrandt and Canaletto
- Extensive grounds, with deer parks and black-horned sheep

- Sea walk; nature trail; formal rose garden; educational day centre
- Stables museum; Family museum

Licensed restaurant; & *partial access*

Open: Easter weekend; 30 Apr–19 Sep, daily

Admission: Adult £2.50; Child £1; *grounds only* Adult £1; Child with parents free

PALACE OF HOLYROODHOUSE

Edinburgh
Tel: 031 556 7371
(at the foot of the Royal Mile)

- Official residence of the Queen when in Scotland
- Ancient origins and lots of fascinating history, involving famous monarchs
- State apartments, house tapestries and paintings
- Picture gallery with portraits of over 70 Scottish kings

Souvenirs; tea room; & *(but ring first)*

Open: 16 May–31 May, 13 Jun–4 Jul, 9–5, Sun 10.30–4.30; Nov–Mar 9.30–3.45 (not Sun)

Admission: Full tour: Adult £1.60; Child/OAP 80p

ROYAL BOTANIC GARDEN

Inverleith Row, Arboretum Road, Edinburgh
Tel: 031 552 7171

- World-famous rock garden
- Probably the biggest collection of rhododendrons in the world
- Unique exhibition of plant houses, with exotic plants

Two tea rooms; publications counter

Open: daily, 9 (Sun 11) to one hour before sunset in summer; 9–dusk in winter; during Edinburgh festival opens at 10 on Sun

Admission: free

STRATHCLYDE

BURNS COTTAGE AND MUSEUM

Alloway
Tel: 0292 41215
(on B7024, 2m S of Ayr)

- Thatched cottage where Robert Burns was born
- Adjoining museum of Burns memorabilia
- Gardens

*Tea room (May–Oct); gift shop; &
partial access*

Open: all year, Jun–Aug 9–7 (Sun 10–7); Apr, May, Sep, Oct, 10–5 (Sun, 2–6); winter 10–4, closed Sun

Admission: Adult £1.20; Child/
OAP 60p (ticket includes *Burns
Monument* nearby)

CULZEAN CASTLE AND COUNTRY PARK

Tel: 06556 274
(A719, 12m SSW of Ayr)

- Splendid 18th-century castle built around ancient tower
- Fine ceilings, oval staircase and Round Drawing Room
- Eisenhower Presentation, explaining his association with castle
- 565-acre Country Park, the first in Scotland

- Reception and Interpretation Centre, with exhibition
- Walled garden; aviary; swan pond; camellia house
- Guided nature walks; talks and films in summer

Licensed self-service restaurant

Open: Apr, Sep, Oct except Easter week, 12–5; 1st May–31st Aug, 10–6; last admission 20 minutes before closing

Admission: Cost of admission of car into the *park* £3.50. Admission into *castle* Adult £2, Child/OAP £1

FINGAL'S CAVE

Staffa
Tel: 0631 63122 or 06885 239
(on the uninhabited island of Staffa seen by steamer and boat trips from Oban and Mull)

- Massive cave flanked by black pillared walls and columns
- Inspiration of Mendelssohn's overture *The Hebrides*

*Catering/bar facilities on Caledonian
MacBrayne steamer; &*

Open: Trips usually available from about Easter (depending on the weather) to end Sep/early Oct

Admission: Different trips have various costs.

GLASGOW ART GALLERY AND MUSEUM

Kelvingrove Park
Tel: 041 357 3929

- Outstanding collection of European paintings
- Sculpture; furniture; silver; pottery; porcelain; armoury; etc.

- Archaeological, historical and ethnographic displays
- Natural history section with dinosaurs, fossils and birds

&

Open: all year, daily, 10–5, Sun 2–5

Admission: free

GLASGOW MUSEUM OF TRANSPORT

Kelvin Hall
Tel: 041 357 3929
(off Argyle Street)

- Large collection of trams, buses, motor cars, horse-drawn vehicles, railway locomotives, fire engines and bikes
- Special displays and models
- Gallery with fine collection of ship models

Self-service tearoom and shop; &

Open: all year, daily, 10–5, Sun 2–5

Admission: free

HAGGS CASTLE

100 St Andrew's Drive, Glasgow
Tel: 041 427 2725

- 16th-century castle, developed as a children's museum of history
- Workshops, with museum-based activities for children every Saturday
- Landscaped gardens, with herb and vegetable plots

Shop; & *partial access*

Open: all year, daily 10–5, Sun 2–5

Admission: free

INVERARAY CASTLE

Tel: 0499 2203
(½m N of Inveraray)

- Seat of the chiefs of Clan Campbell, then Dukes of Argyll
- Impressive interior with portraits, relics, armoury and more
- Gardens open on selected weekends

Tea room and craft shop; & *partial access*

Open: 2 Apr–9 Oct, 10–12.30, 2–6 Mon–Thur; Sat, Sun 2–6; closed Fri

Admission: Adult £2.20; Child £1.10; OAP £1.70

TAYSIDE

BLAIR CASTLE

Tel: 079 681 355
(just off the main Perth–Inverness Road (A9), 35m N of Perth)

- White-turreted baronial castle, seat of the Earls and Dukes of Atholl (the only British subject allowed to maintain a private army)
- Fine furniture; portraits; lace; china; armoury; relics
- Cumming's Tower dating from 1269
- Deer park; pony-trekking; nature trails

Licensed restaurant; gift shop; picnic areas; &

Open: 31 Mar–end Oct, Mon–Sat 10–6, Sun 2–6 (except Jul and Aug, 12–6); last admission 5

Admission: Adult £2.50; OAP £2.00; Child £1.50; *Family Ticket* £7.50

INDEX OF ATTRACTIONS

Design: Sue Storey
Maps: David Perrott
Typeset by Goodfellow & Egan, Cambridge
Printed and bound in Spain
by Cayfosa, Barcelona